NO MAN IS AN ISLAND

NO MAN IS AN ISLAND

ROGER RAWCLIFFE

MANX HERITAGE FOUNDATION

First published by the Manx Heritage Foundation 2009
PO Box 1986, Douglas, Isle of Man IM99 1SR

Printed and bound in Wales by Gomer Press Limited, Ceredigion

Cover design: Ruth Sutherland

British Library Cataloguing in Publication Data
A catalogue record for this book is available from the British Library

ISBN 978-0-9554043-2-0

To those who have come to share in the life of the
Isle of Man, and to those who have welcomed them.

CHAPTER 10
'O Land Of Our Birth'

CHAPTER 11
The Transformation of the Landscape

CHAPTER 12
But Man Is An Island

CHAPTER 13
Or Is It? - A Postscript

ILLUSTRATIONS

INTRODUCTION

It is now forty-eight years since Sir Ronald Garvey announced the abolition of surtax. It was felt that an account of the consequences of this momentous step, particularly as regards the development of the finance sector in the Isle of Man, should be written while many of those involved were still able to remember the various stages and often colourful events which accompanied it. The Manx Heritage Foundation therefore commissioned me to write a book on this period. I felt that this history should be placed in the context of the Island's history, at any rate in the way in which the Island has been able to exploit its position in the centre of the Irish Sea and the British Isles and its advantageous constitutional status as a separate jurisdiction, at any rate since the late seventeenth century.

There may be many others who could be more appropriate to compile this book; however, I have lived and worked here for the past thirty years, much of the time for the leading accounting firm of Pannell Kerr Forster which was government auditor up to the late 1980s as well as the auditor not only of many of the major Manx businesses, but also of a large number of the new banks and insurance companies and was therefore at the centre of events in the sector. My connection with the Island goes back to my birth, receiving, a week after birth, my first postcard, of the Point of Ayre lighthouse, from my father at TA camp at Milntown; I could see the Island on clear evenings from school at Fleetwood during the war; we had a wonderful holiday in Port Erin in 1948, and I have been coming here several times a year since my engagement in 1959, acquiring a cottage in 1968. So that, even if I was not living here in the 1960s and 1970s, I was partly aware of what was happening even before coming permanently at the end of 1979. In addition to this, I have been responsible for the module on the economic history of the Isle of Man for the Centre for Manx Studies, contributed to the financial services aspects of the economic history chapter for Volume 5 of the *New History of the Isle of Man*, delivered a paper on the history of the accountancy profession in the Island to the Natural History and Antiquarian Society, and commissioned and been co-author of *A Time of Manx Cheer – a History of the Licensed Trade in the Isle of Man*.

My brief has been to produce a readable and accessible account, to include some of the colourful stories and characters of the period and a flavour of the strong opposition to the new industry on the part of groups of Manx nationalists. I have interviewed many of the main personalities closely connected with the activities of the sector, particularly up to the events surrounding the collapse of the Savings and Investments Bank and its aftermath; and with its development and control both before and after that event. There could have been very many more people who could have been interviewed, but the selection that was made covered most of the ground. The names of those who helped in this way can be found at the back of the book.

Likewise the book was not to be a technical history; to have made it so would have required a far mightier volume, and, in any case, much of the ground has been covered in specialist volumes, many written in the series by Mark Solly. Some references are made to legislation or definitions of law or of tax where is seemed necessary as explanation of the narrative for the benefit of the general reader.

The book is intended to give a balanced view of the period both in its narrative and its opinions. The 'credit crunch' of 2008 brought serious problems to the Island, and necessitated an extra postscript chapter modifying the optimistic conclusion of the books as written in 2007. Nevertheless I remain broadly optimistic. Any failure of balance, omissions or errors, are mine.

I want to thank all those who have helped with the preparation of the book; first the contributors already referred to; next and most important, Sue Lewis who helped with a great deal of the factual research, produced most of the quotations from the nineteenth century and was the major source for Chapter 10 on the subject of the reaction of the Manx to the new developments, an important theme of the book; Maureen Harris who has translated my handwriting into the type which appears; Charles Guard who, as Administrator of the Manx Heritage Foundation commissioned the book, helped with interviews after the departure of Sue Lewis, edited and published it; John Hall for his photographs, particularly of the buildings.

CHAPTER 1

NO MAN IS AN ISLAND

But it helps! The Isle of Man, like its neighbours England, Ireland, Scotland and Wales, has throughout its history been affected, not only by those neighbours, but by influences from further afield, most importantly the Norse Vikings. As is well known, the Island sits in the middle of the Irish Sea at the geographical centre of the British Isles but unlike many other British islands it is distinct and not part of a group. Although its earliest history, especially during the Roman occupation of Britain, is largely unknown, it joined in the flourishing period set off by Celtic Christianity from the fifth or sixth centuries.

It is probable that, through all the history of immigration and emigration, the racial composition of the Manx, as shown by admittedly limited tests, is similar to those of the inhabitants of the neighbouring islands, even to that of the most diverse, England. Immigration and intermarriage, even during periods of new settlement, have not radically undermined the nature of the original inhabitants despite the arrival of a limited number of Romans, rather more Anglo-Saxons, Vikings, Norse and Danes, and subsequent refugees. These original people are thought of as Celtic, but even these were far from homogeneous ranging from short dark people to tall, fair, sometimes red headed people, all of which can be seen among the modern population. The common trait of these early inhabitants lay in the use of Celtic languages, customs and art forms, and these persisted in the Isle of Man as well as in Ireland, Wales and parts of Scotland. In the 19th century there was a revival of interest and enthusiasm for the Celtic cultures, not least more recently in the Isle of Man.

Into this world came the Norsemen, and their discovery of the Island was a crucial factor in its later independence. Sailing round the north of Scotland southward into the Irish Sea from the eighth century the

Norsemen founded new settlements in western Scotland, Ireland, North West England, and the Isle of Man. Quickly recognising the Island's strategic importance, they made it a base for plundering expeditions and later the administrative base for their Kingdom of Man and the Isles; this was one of the most distinctive and long-lasting of the Norse satellite kingdoms whose ultimate sovereign was the King of Norway. An essential feature of Norse life was the annual open-air assembly, or Thing, and such an assembly was established on the Island a thousand years ago and, remarkably, still functions today. Now known as Tynwald, this parliamentary system lies at the heart of Manx independence and nationhood and represents the oldest continuous parliament in the world, holdings its annual open air meeting every July 5th, Tynwald Day, for the purpose of promulgating new laws which have been passed by the regular meetings of Tynwald throughout the year.[1]

It is this feature, above all, that has preserved the distinctiveness that has enabled the Isle of Man to retain not only its sense of nationhood but also the political separateness needed as a basis for its development. Other British islands such as the Isle of Wight, Anglesey, the Western Isles or Orkney and Shetland, all of which share parts of the general history of the region, have not had the freedom to develop in the same way as the Isle of Man which, especially in latter years, has used this freedom to offer specialist services for which there is a worldwide market. Only the Channel Islands, whose history as the remnant of Duke William's Duchy of Normandy is also distinct, have been able also to exploit their differences. They have the advantage of better accessibility than the Isle of Man, especially to the continent, but perhaps a lesser sense of nationhood than the Island; nor do they have the distinct framework of political institutions and of customary law, which the Isle of Man has in common with England. The Channel Island philosophy of law is closer to that of the Continent which has meant that they have had to introduce much of their compatibility to English law by statute, particularly for the purposes of financial services.

The Island's geographical and political distinctiveness have made easier a sense of nationhood. The Isle of Man can reasonably claim a national identity as distinct as those of the surrounding four nations of the British Isles, albeit on a tiny scale. The grounds for such a claim are clearly identifiable. It has its own history that did not concern itself particularly with its neighbours, at any rate up to the Tudor period. Its political institutions have remained in existence for over a thousand years, governing the Island and creating and interpreting its laws, even if not always very actively until recent centuries. It has its own language, if not much literature, and like its language the source of its indigenous people is initially Celtic. Like its neighbours in the British Isles it has regularly absorbed newcomers: Norsemen, followed by the English during the Stanleys' rule, and in the last two centuries more widely from the British Isles, though predominantly from England. Inevitably for several centuries there has been some process of Anglicisation, not only in the adoption of English as the first language of virtually all Manxmen, but in the feeling of being part of the greater British nation which, for two hundred years, has shared in the benefits of trade, enterprise and settlement encompassed in the period of the British Empire. An example of the Island's identification with Britishness is the huge contribution made by the Manx in two World Wars, notably by the Manx Regiment in the Second World War; this was out of all proportion to the size of the population. This sense of identification with Britishness characterised the nations of the British Isles, except perhaps the majority of Irishmen, until the recent upsurge of petty nationalism, once evident only in the domain of sport, but which now threatens to dissolve the Union which has served so well.

Despite this close association with Britain, the Isle of Man has never been part of the Union or the United Kingdom. Although the Norse Kingdom was subsumed into the sovereignty of England, with the King (or Queen) of England as the supreme authority, the granting of the Island as an almost separate kingdom to the Stanleys in 1405, ensured a separateness which provided opportunities to develop a distinct political regime and other trading possibilities which would have been impossible had the Island been part of the United Kingdom. Even after the Revestment Act of 1765 when the King of England (by now the King of the United Kingdom) took back the Kingship of Man, (though by now described as the Lordship of Man), the Island remained separate, and although Revestment introduced a period of some two hundred years during which the United Kingdom ruled and controlled the Island's resources through a series of Lieutenant Governors appointed by the UK, the governors still had to act through Tynwald. Gradually the purse strings have been loosened and, from the time of Governor Loch in the 1860s, political and fiscal control have progressively reverted to Tynwald.

In the course of the previous century, the British Government not only imposed increasingly heavy customs duties on the Island, but also retained any surplus for its own purposes. This situation continued until the advent of Governor Loch in 1863, after which a radical change was brought about. The reform of the House of Keys and the question of financial control were settled in 1866, when an Isle of Man Customs and Harbours Act was passed by Westminster, and a House of Keys Election Act was passed by Tynwald. The Island gained the benefit of surplus insular revenue, after the payment to the British Government of an annual fixed contribution of £10,000. Since that date the Island has levied its own taxes and controlled its own financial affairs although, under the Customs Agreement of 1957, the Island agreed, with minor exceptions, to keep all the indirect taxes at the same levels as in Britain. Almost a century later, the UK's Isle of Man Act of 1958 ushered in a new period of internal self-government. Although the UK Government retains the right to withhold the Royal Assent to a Bill of Tynwald, this Act, subject to pressure emanating from international bodies such as the EU or OECD, allows the Island to make the best use of its distinctive status. The Isle of Man Act formed the point of departure for the changes introduced in 1960, which are the principal focus of this book.

Since the introduction of income tax in the Isle of Man in 1918, the buoyancy of its customs revenues had enabled the Isle of Man to manage with much lower rates of income tax than the United Kingdom, ranging from 7.5 to 13.125 %. In 1938/9, surtax[2] was introduced in the Isle of Man on incomes over £2,000. The proposal for the abolition of this surtax in 1960 gave rise to much debate in the Island in which anxieties about possible detrimental effects on the Island's way of life featured largely.

Tourism and the TT races had long formed part of the traditional Manx way of life. They had, moreover, become associated with the Island in the consciousness of people outside its shores, along with more fundamental elements such as Tynwald and the Island's unique system of Government. Yet, when tourism was introduced in the nineteenth century, critical voices were raised expressing concern about the impact on the 'Manx way of life'; yet 'the season' and the 'visitors' are now thought of as typical of the 'Manx way of life', just as, a little later, the Island's name was to become synonymous with motorcycle racing. Perhaps in fifty years' time it will be the financial sector, shipping register and the film industry which Manx Nationalists will be vociferously defending as part of the Island's traditional heritage.

For any discussion of the Island's unique cultural and political nature it is necessary to consider the question of Manxness and the Manx. One of the features of the influx of new residents and the growth of the finance sector in the latter part of the 20th century has been the reawakening of Manx consciousness and nationalism, especially in the 1970s and again from 1987. This was accompanied by a revival of use of the Manx Gaelic language and of cultural manifestations of music, dancing and literature. This revival often met with the disapproval of older Manx people of unassailable Manx descent, since the new national awareness was accompanied by outright hostility to arrivals from other parts of Britain. The figures shown by successive censuses of the proportion of persons born in the Island were eagerly seized upon to demonstrate the rape of the Island by unsympathetic arrivals.[3] However, the picture is more complex as many of those recorded as born in the Island are the children of the wider British and others now working in the Island, and a considerable number of returning people of Manx ancestry, will form part of those shown in the census as born elsewhere. But the broader sweep of history shows a continuous process. Families that have settled in the Island as a consequence of earlier influxes, as when the Stanleys became Kings of Man, or with the growth of the tourist industry in the second half of the nineteenth century, have long since been

accepted as Manx, and names that were once new to the Island such as
Stowell or Radcliffe, are now regarded as 'Manx as the hills'. This
discussion illustrates the futility of the narrow nationalist argument. But
a proper regard and respect for the Manx nation (however one chooses to
define the term) should be shown by all who have made the commitment
to live and work in the Isle of Man. Without the new residents the Island's
population would probably have amounted to no more than 30,000.

Some of the anxieties about an uncontrollable influx of new residents
were articulated in the debates on the proposed abolition of surtax in
1960. However, the facts of the matter were that, since the Island's main
economic pillar, tourism, was in inevitable decline, the Island had to take
urgent steps to avert bankruptcy. Even as late as at the time of the arrival
of Bill Dawson as Treasurer of the Isle of Man in 1969, the Governor,
Sir Peter Stallard and John Bolton the Chairman of the Finance Board,
had grave anxieties about the Island's long term solvency as they briefed
him to develop financial services as a future money earner for the Island.
Like the UK, the Island had taken on the full burden of the National
Health Service and Social Security protection in 1948 and this needed
strong finances to pay for it. In addition there was a need to expand the
Island's infrastructure to meet a growing population and provide the
considerable funds required to modernize utilities that had been installed
largely a century or more earlier. Modern safety and health requirements
had to be met as well as the need to upgrade the hospital and schools. If
the answer to the Island's pressing financial problems given by some of
the Manx nationalists had been adopted, to support tourism by
government finance, there is little doubt that the funds would not have
been available to support even a modest standard of living for Islanders;
and the aspiration that a quiet but virtuously Manx way of life based on
simple pleasures and modest demands, few facilities and a diet of the
proverbial spuds and herrings would be preferable to the influx of new
workers and new businesses, does not bear serious examination. The
likely consequence of this policy would have been that the Island would
have become an economic backwater bringing about its absorption into
England, and Tynwald being abolished to be replaced by one MP at

Westminster, and likewise into the European Union. It would have lost control of its own destiny for ever.

Certainly there have been problems associated with the growth both of the Island's financial services and with residents seeking protection from excessive taxes elsewhere. Some of the earlier new residents behaved arrogantly and insensitively towards the Manx and demands have been made on undeveloped countryside for building houses. In fact demands on the infrastructure have been heavy, even if some of those demands would have arisen in any case. And there is no doubt that the reputation of the Island has sometimes suffered, as with the collapse of the Savings and Investment Bank in 1982, though the reputational damage attached to the recent Manx Electricity Authority loans is not a function of the new activities and has been fanned by those seeking to discredit their political opponents, including by nationalist spokesmen, at the expense of the Island's good name. Whether the 'quality of life' of the Island, so often mentioned by politicians, has improved or suffered is largely a matter of opinion or temperament. There might even be a prejudice about this in certain quarters to prove a point and to support the condemnation of what has happened, particularly the successful development of the Island's financial services, which were the indirect consequences of the abolition of surtax that lie at the heart of this study.

But no man is an Island and no one owes us a living. We have to live with our neighbours and trade with our neighbours to increase our nation's wealth. There is no shame in success in commerce if conducted with integrity. The Island's gross domestic product per caput has risen from far below that of the UK to slightly above the UK at the time of writing.[4] This is a real and substantial achievement which came about as a result of a bold and original idea, the abolition of surtax, from which flowed the growth of new residents and the building up of the Island's financial services industry in all its forms. The successive governors from Sir Ambrose Dundas to the present have each taken the process a little further. There have been tensions and protests; there have been hiccoughs as a consequence of government errors as well as world economic circumstances; but in general it is a story of politicians, civil servants and those who work on the Island co-operating to make steady progress over a period of almost half a century. This book seeks to provide an account of that period.

CHAPTER 2

SET IN THE SEA

Before the Revestment Act of 1765, the Isle of Man had suffered little direct interference from the English or British Government, although there had for a century been some pressure on the Lords of Man to curtail the irritation of smuggling. There had also been successive waves of new residents who came to the Island for economic and political reasons. One such wave was associated with the start of the rule of the Stanleys.

When Sir John Stanley was granted the Kingship of the Island in 1405, he, and subsequently his successors, put in place an administrative system which comprised officials and a certain number of soldiery, many of whom were brought in from England, the majority from the Stanleys' own lands in Lancashire. The seat of Island government at this time was Castletown and the rent-roll of 1643 lists some 392 tenants, of whom virtually half bear names of non-Manx origin, indicating that even by this time there had been a substantial influx of new families.

Many names appear which have since become to be thought of as Manx (and may, after 500 years, reasonably be so regarded), such as Radcliffe, first recorded in 1496, Skillicorn (1511), Maddrell (1499), Sayle (1490)[5]. But the number of people of English origin who came to occupy positions of authority in the Island was significant. This flood of new arrivals long foreshadowed the influx of tradesmen and businessmen which would be seen in the expansion of the nineteenth century, and of finance sector employees in the twentieth century.

Running Trade

The first of the activities to exploit successfully the special political and administrative status of the Isle of Man as an independent petty kingdom was the 'running trade', regarded as a legitimate business by the Islanders, but condemned as smuggling by the English. This activity

Bridge House, Castletown. Home of Quayle's Bank and associated with the era of smuggling. It has its own ingenious strongroom. It was the first office of Lloyd's Life and is still used as offices.

began in the second half of the seventeenth century. Up to that time, evidence suggests that the economy of the Island was at or near subsistence level, dependent upon farming and fishing, with craftsmen producing the simple necessities of life. Most housing was simple and basic; productive activities consisted of milling, baking, brewing, mostly small scale or home produced, carpentry, building and weaving.

One of the consequences of the English Navigation Acts of 1660 and 1671 was the restriction on exports of cattle from the Island to England. The same Acts gave the English Government direct administration of customs revenue. The Navigation Acts of 1651 and 1660 had restricted trade between England and the Baltic and the Eastern Mediterranean, and the 1660 Act ruled that colonial products, including tobacco, sugar and liquor, had to be carried in English, Welsh or Irish vessels and landed in those countries whatever the ultimate destination of the cargo. Whatever the detail of these Acts, the Isle of Man lay outside this jurisdiction. Vessels could land goods in Manx harbours if (the considerably lower) Manx import and anchorage duties were paid. These duties were legitimately levied by the Isle of Man at a much lower level, as the Island was entirely responsible for its own taxes and duties. Of course, such low import duties on an island so close to British and Irish shores was an open invitation to those entrepreneurs who could then arrange for the clandestine delivery of these goods to neighbouring lands where no further duties were paid. In a further twist, some commodities, such as tobacco, were landed and paid duty in England, then re-exported to the Island with rebates of customs duty, quite legally. These, along with others originally landed on the Island, were then run back into England, Scotland or Ireland in small quantities illegally, thus avoiding the full duty. A rise in duty in 1679 from 5% to 10% and an embargo on French goods increased the financial incentives for Manx smugglers and their agents.

The slave trade also gave opportunities for the importation of tobacco, sugar and liquor on ships that had sailed from English ports like Liverpool, carrying a cargo of goods which were then traded in West Africa for slaves. The vessels then returned from the West Indies carrying a cargo of dutiable goods to the Island. Here the cargo was broken down into smaller, more manageable loads to run across to North-west England. Bridge House in Castletown and the adjacent historic 'Peggy' boathouse bear witness to the success of one local family, the Quayles, who profited sufficiently from this trade to be able to establish one of the Island's first banks. Enraged by the loss of revenue in customs dues, (and one estimate put the annual figure in the 1750s at £100m in today's money), the British Government attempted to persuade the Island's hereditary rulers, the Earls of Derby and later the Dukes of Atholl, to curtail this activity, but without much success.

In the early part of the 18th century the British Government had made little attempt to fulfil its undertaking to allow free export of Manx cattle and goods into Britain. Possibly this intransigence had made the Atholls disinclined to oblige them by making any serious effort to curb the running trade in view of the inevitable poverty which would have resulted in the Island and the loss of revenue which its Lord must consequently experience, and British pressure on the 2nd Duke of Atholl had not been successful, but after his death in 1764, the 3rd Duke was finally prevailed upon to sell the royalties and rights to the Island's revenues back to the British Crown for £70,000. This was done by Act of Parliament in the Revestment Act of 1765, without reference to Tynwald.

For a hundred years after Revestment little of the surplus revenue of the Island was returned to it for its betterment. After 1765 the majority of the non-Manx participants in the running trade, known as 'merchant strangers', appear to have left the scene forthwith[6]. Although now illegal under Manx as well as British law, the running trade did not cease immediately, but it dwindled and eventually died out. About ten per cent of the organisers of the running trade had been Manx and within the Island the trade had been considered an honourable occupation. No stigma was attached to those engaged in it, nor was there much serious effort to curb an activity that broke no Manx laws. The trade had lasted for more than 100 years, and the wealth it generated for the Island enriched the Lords of Man as well as the principals of the trade, who acquired shipping and banking interests on the strength of it. Some measure of prosperity cascaded down to the ordinary Manxmen who handled the goods and manned the ships.

Although the running trade was at odds with British legislation it was merely exploiting an anomaly in the Island's status, which placed it outside the jurisdiction of the United Kingdom of Britain and Ireland. By the time it eventually died out completely during the early part of the 19th century, the anomaly of the Island's status had already been providing a further opportunity for making money: the attraction of new residents in the form of defaulting debtors.

Debtors and Half-pay Officers

In 1743, William Murrey, a merchant of Douglas, states that the running trade had been 'aggravated' by the clause in the Act of 1737 which 'virtually gave persons coming to reside in Man immunity from all debts contracted elsewhere.'[7] The French Revolution and the Napoleonic wars had made fleeing one's creditors to the Continent, the traditional refuge for English and Irish debtors, an unappealing and perilous option. Tynwald's

Statute Law Act of 1737 in effect provided protection to insolvent debtors who came to the Isle of Man: it made it impossible for creditors outside the Island to seize the goods of debtors that were located within the Island, or for debtors to be pursued on the Island for debts contracted elsewhere. The Act was repealed in 1814, but in the meantime the Isle of Man had attracted a considerable number of new residents in the form of insolvent debtors who were making the most of the distinctive status of the Island. These newcomers were not universally beloved:

> Many of this class were of extravagant habits and of doubtful character; this led to great excess and frequent quarrels towards the end of the last century and the commencement of the present. A law was consequently promulgated on the 24 March 1814, being 'An Act for the more easy recovery of debts contracted out of the limits of the Isle of Man'. This was looked upon by many as ruinous to the best interests of the Island, but the result proved the contrary.[8]

The writer of the following lines, a Miss Gulindo, was no doubt one who availed herself of the Island's advantages:

> Welcome! Welcome! Brother debtor,
> To this poor but happy place,
> Where no bailiff dun, or gaoler,
> Dares to show his dreadful face.

Mrs Hannah Bullock, who resided in the Island at the time, gives a graphic account of the doings of these gentry:[9] Although published in 1816, some of her remarks have an uncanny resonance with the attitudes of some of the incomers the Island was to see nearly 150 years later in the 1960s:

> In the minds of those who have thought of this place at all, a strong prejudice has hitherto existed against it, as a mere asylum where debtors might elude the claims of their creditors! That the protection hitherto granted by the laws of the island, has in many instances invited the unprincipled and extravagant to a temporary residence, cannot be denied; but... it has afforded a retreat, where by the practice of economy those affairs have been retrieved, and debts paid, which had the individuals been subjected to imprisonment, with its attendant disadvantages and expenses, never would have been effected...

The insular legislature, influenced by a requisition, from the British
government, have thrown open a door to the recovery of foreign
debts; and the consequences of this act are, for the present, most
seriously felt in the island, where the sums brought in by strangers,
increased the circulation, and gave the necessary stimulus to
commerce and agriculture; ... the island presents advantages
nowhere else to be found in the United Kingdom.

Although the number of debt refugees does not appear to have been
great, Bullock notes that they seem to have considerably annoyed the local
inhabitants with their affectations of wealth and manners. Again, many of
these sentiments could equally have applied to the Island in the 1960s and '70s:

....those who have come hither from other countries have seldom
presented good specimens; the most striking traits exhibited ... have
been a sovereign contempt for those they came to live amongst, a
prodigious flippancy, vast affectation of high breeding, and
pretensions to a rank in their own country, not always borne out by
facts. ... it was usual to pass their time in querulous regret at the fate
which had condemned them to irradiate so low a sphere, and eager
anticipations of their return to a more extended circle. The ill policy
of shewing this aversion to the retreat they had chosen, must be
plain to any comprehension! No one returns esteem for contempt,
and nothing could be more natural than to join in the regret thus
loudly expressed, that fortune had compelled them to take a station
in society, where they were neither welcome or invited guests.
...At first, ... the natives, dazzled by the polished manners and
superior acquirements of their visitors, opened their hearts and their
houses to them; but this cordiality was short lived. Gold had, at this
time, become one of the household gods of the Manx, ... hence
arose suspicion on one side, and contempt on the other; so that, at
last, both parties drew off into separate associations, and all chance
of conciliation was at an end. ... I was both astonished and alarmed
at the enmity then existing between them. The weekly paper was the
instrument of war...
The Manx continually threatened to withdraw the protection
afforded to these interlopers, who in their turn warned them, that
the island would be ruined by such a measure: they insisted that all

St. Mary's garrison church, Castletown. Formerly the garrison church for the government and officers. It was converted into offices for Canada Life International.

the prosperity of the country originated with them! That it was supported by their money, and might be civilised by their example; ... anyone would have supposed these were a class of missionaries who had made a pilgrimage, with the disinterested view of diffusing light and wealth, whilst the Manx as sturdily denied the benefit, and expressed their wish to be left in mediocrity and ignorance, rather than be annoyed by the airs of superiority assumed over them.

At the height of this hostility, public attention was diverted by the arrival of Irish duellists, which briefly cast the whole Island into a ferment. The presence of pugnacious Irishmen and of insolvent debtors overlapped with the arrival of impoverished English gentlefolk from England, who had discovered that they could keep up appearances and a certain standard of living more easily in the Isle of Man, with its lower costs and taxes, than at home.

The same applied to unemployed officers on half pay. During the eighteenth century, the armed forces, especially the Royal Navy, had moved away from a policy of recruiting additional officers on contracts when the situation demanded, to one of retaining officers in reserve on half-pay. The new system was in operation from the middle of the eighteenth century, but, for half-pay officers, as for debtors, the French revolution, followed by the Napoleonic wars, meant that living on the Continent ceased to be an option. A large number of half-pay officers settled in the Isle of Man. Though not rich, they liked to maintain a certain life style. They too brought money to the Island, but not in profusion, and their influence was not always beneficial. The affectations of some new residents are summed up in an undated cutting from the *Morning Herald*:

> The puny Ensign, puffed with punch and beer, who struts and starves on forty pounds a year, elsewhere becomes ennobled when he touches this fair isle - talks of his old port, and invites you to imbibe his Chateau Margaux!

Nor did the pretensions of the English incomers go down well with the Manx, either. David Robinson in his *Tour Through the Isle of Man* stated:

> The harmony of society in Douglas is sometimes marred by mutual prejudices. In many of the natives, notwithstanding a show of politeness and hospitality, there is secret aversion to strangers; and in several of the English an unreasonable contempt of the Manks.

These and the following words could have been reasonably written in the years after 1960, too. John Stowell, under his pen-name 'Tom the Gardener', comments on the detrimental effects of the changes in Douglas society, brought about by the bad influence of half-pay officers and other new residents, on the town's young ladies:[10]

> Ask not from whence my little Daphne came;
> A gay coquette is ev'ry way the same;
> Manks born, Manks bred, Manks made, Manks fed, Manks taught;
> She's Manks is every thing but what she ought.
> Pray what is that? In modesty and sense:
> Virtues, alas! too long departed hence.
> Daphne would fain disown from whence she sprung.

Loch Promenade, Douglas. The long sweep of Loch Promenade was built around 1877 on reclaimed land speculatively by Alexander Gill. This section of the promenade is still almost complete, and depends for its effect on the repetition of its Victorian façades rather than individual quality. The first hotel in the terrace, Admiral House, was lavishly refurbished at the expense of the Savings and Investment Bank.

Tourism

During this same period, around the beginning of the nineteenth century, the Island began to draw increasing numbers of a more salubrious type of stranger: summer visitors. In 1811 George Woods wrote:

> On its being the continual resort of strangers depends, and I think may safely depend, the increasing prosperity of this country. [11]

Figures of arrivals by sea show a steady increase during the 19th and early 20th centuries. Even as early as the 1830s, arrival figures reached 20,000, rising to 50,000 by the 1850s, while in 1880 the number rose to 92,765 (by comparison, in the 1830s Blackpool attracted a mere 1000 visitors), and by 1913 it was over 660,000. Visitor numbers naturally dropped during the two wars, although the use of the Island for prisoners, detainees or military activities, especially the internment of enemy aliens,

The Central Hotel, Douglas.
Recently restored and converted into flats, it provides a striking contrast in
the middle of Central Promenade. Built around 1890.

replaced much of the income lost from the temporary suspension of the
tourist industry; but after the wars, the figures recovered.

Although most of the new visitors were workers from the industrial
towns of northern England or Scotland who came to the Island to spend
their annual holiday, or 'wakes' weeks, these were not the only kind of
holiday-makers. Wealthier families acquired holiday homes where the
wives and children could spend the summer, while the husbands could
join them at the weekends. A notable example of this is the Colony at

The Ridgeway, Douglas, of 1895. Recently converted into offices for advocates Simcocks, by Roy Kermode and Bryan Stott.

Port e Vullen which was built by the Groves family, of the Manchester brewers Groves and Whitnall. The colony comprised one large house and half a dozen smaller houses for the younger generation, all set above the sea on a headland in a private estate (and occupied in part by the family right up to 1980).

Visitors were attracted to the Island because it was perceived as unusual and delightful. The appeal for holiday-makers lay in the adventure of a sea journey from Liverpool or Fleetwood, Llandudno, Dublin, Belfast or Glasgow, and the exotic destination with its scenery, interest and amenities. The newly-built accommodation in Douglas, Ramsey or Port Erin was modern, the Island was beautiful with its hills, glens and

The Mooragh Promenade, Rasmey. A promenade hotel development similar to those in Douglas which was never completed.

beaches and its gardens fringed with palm trees. New places of entertainment proliferated, offering shows featuring the leading stars of the day. The Isle of Man is celebrated in many nineteenth-century music hall songs which capture something of the atmosphere of frolic and fun. Visitors could explore the Island by steam trains, or electric trams running along coasts and up the mountain, while, early in the 20th century, the ubiquitous *char-à-banc* was to make its appearance. The famous motor car and motorcycle races, still held today, were introduced at this period.

The Spectator offered A London View of the Isle of Man 1880

The Isle of Man is but little known to the higher classes of holidaymakers, though it is annually visited by many thousands of strangers. Those who flock thither are almost all persons of the lower middle class, and operatives from the thickly-populated towns

Bradda Mount, Douglas. Typical terraced houses in Upper Douglas, built on open ground during the expansion of the town around the end of the 19th century.

of Lancashire and Yorkshire. ... But the Isle of Man may fairly claim a visit from persons of higher culture than these. Regarded simply as a health resort, there can be no question that it is the most thorough sea residence in the kingdom, On every side is the sea, and from whatever quarter of the compass the wind chooses to blow it comes from the sea, and there is scarcely a spot ... unless it be some narrow inland glen, from which the ocean in its various moods cannot be seen. .... The sea views are, in fact, perhaps more striking than in any part of the United Kingdom, except the north-west coast of Scotland. But in the Isle of Man they are broader and almost as bold; the rugged masses of Spanish Head, the mellow colouring of the Calf, and the wide expanse of waters on every side, dotted by scores of herring boats, is a scene which in its breadth is unequalled on any of our coasts. The absence of trees renders the land views cold and harsh, but it is the general coast views, the glens and coves which open to the sea, which are the characteristic and charming portion of Manx scenery; whilst the genial winters and cool summers produce some vegetation quite abnormal in this latitude. There are dozens of cottages protected by high hedges of fuchsias - one mass of bright, hanging flowers - whilst the delicate veronica flourishes in shrubs six feet in height.

Devonshire Crescent, Douglas. Further development of the town in open fields between the wars.

Although the new arrivals provided seasonal work for Manx people and a steady demand for the produce of the land and sea, the visiting trade was not universally welcomed outside of Douglas. In Hall Caine's novel *The Manxman* (1894), the Manx people are represented as resenting the tourists, and complaining about all the money being spent for the benefit of the visiting trade, particularly in Douglas, rather than on harbours and breakwaters for the local fishermen. In the novel, as in the Hitchcock film of the same name, the fishermen present a petition to Tynwald, appealing against the proposed imposition of harbour dues for facilities they felt to be inadequate. Hall Caine represents them expressing themselves in phrases which might echo those of the 1970s and 1980s, thus 'With the farming going to the dogs and the fishing going to the divil, d'ye know what our ould island's coming to? It's coming to an island of lodging-house keepers and hackney-car drivers. Not the Isle of Man at all, but the Isle of Manchester.' The complaints had some justification - much more so than similar complaints relating to expenditure on the Finance Sector in the 1980s or 1990s. But it was essential, for the benefit of the Island generally and for the safety of Islanders, visitors, and supplies being brought ashore, to ensure direct landing onto piers at all stages of the tide and, as far as possible, in all weathers. The opening of the Red Pier in Douglas in 1802 was a start, but at most states of the tide visitors and their luggage still had to be transferred from the larger boats anchored in the bay to rowing boats, a daunting experience; it was not until 1872, with the completion of the first part of the Queen Victoria Pier, that larger vessels were able to berth alongside at all states of the tide.

The other requirement for the success of the tourist industry was the establishment of a regular and reliable ferry service. After some rivalry between competitors, this was assured in 1830 with the establishment of what has been known since 1832 as the Isle of Man Steam Packet Company.

The arrival of increasing numbers of visitors necessitated the provision of accommodation and other facilities, the majority of which were based in Douglas. In addition to the piers, new promenades were built on reclaimed land around Douglas Bay: Harris Promenade in the 1860s, and Loch Promenade, completed in 1877 connected to the new pier and to a new main street, Victoria Street. For these two developments, W. J. Rennison designed a range of hotels, from the Villiers, completed in 1878 to the Sefton in 1895. By 1890, the promenade was completed with the building of Queen's Promenade. The horse tramways were laid along Douglas Bay in 1876, and the electric tramway to Laxey in 1894, extended to Ramsey in 1898. The tramway to the summit of Snaefell, laid in 1896, was the only electric mountain tramway in Britain. A steam railway system was already in place as a result of the foundation of the Isle of Man Steam Railway Company in 1870, and other transport systems for the entertainment of visitors had been installed. In addition, grand new places of entertainment were built, almost all of them in Douglas, including four large dance halls (Derby Castle, Falcon Cliff, Marina Pavilion, later converted into the Gaiety Theatre, and the Palace Pavilion), and, later, Noble's Baths and numerous cinemas. Many of these installations still survived in 1960, but by then many of them were in a parlous state.

The expansion of the visiting trade called for enormous capital expenditure. Entrepreneurs like Alexander Gill, who owned some 150 of the new hotels, financed much of the development, and there was considerable speculation in property, as was to happen again in the years following 1960. One of the groups was the Manx-based 'Manx Syndicate', formed around 1888 under the leadership of newspaper owner J. A. Brown. This group was also later involved in the Isle of Man Tramways and Electric Power Company and the ill-fated Brewery Amalgamation, and was financed in part by Dumbell's Bank. The Syndicate built, *inter alia*, over 130 houses speculatively, ready for occupation in 1889, though many remained untenanted.

The 1881 census shows that most of the workforce was drawn from the local Manx community: 92% of masons, joiners 88%, plasterers 83%, and plumbers 73%. However, many of the new hotelkeepers came from outside the Island, mostly from Lancashire, and thus represented another significant influx from England. By 1960, the majority of their descendents had come to be regarded as Manx. In addition, many of the businesses established from the middle of the 19th century were set up by new arrivals or their children; many of these businesses are today regarded as Manx, except perhaps by purists. Many of the people prominent in the Island's business community at the end of the century had non-Manx names: J. A. Brown, Samuel Norris, G. H. Wood, Dr Henry Okell, Henry Brearley, and the Bregazzi, Felice, Newby, Bucknall, Webb, and Earnshaw families. Many of those whose biographies appear in the *New Manx Worthies* (2006) bore names that were not Manx in origin. Over a century later, these families are well assimilated into the community and widely accepted as Manx. In a majority of cases they have married people of Manx origin.

Emigration and Economic Difficulties

However, not all Manx people could find an outlet for their ambition on the Island, as the story of 'Diamond Joe' Mylchreest, who made his fortune ultimately at Kimberley in South Africa, was to show. A similar story is the theme of Hall Caine's *The Manxman*. Those who stayed behind expressed their feelings: 'But the boys - where's the Manx boys at all? Gone like a flight of birds to Austrillya [sic] and Cape and I don't know where. Not a Manx house now that hasn't one of the boys foreign.'

The turn of the twentieth century saw the collapse of Dumbell'
Bank, an event which in some respects foreshadowed the dramatic even s
of the 1980s, with one significant difference: Dumbell's was used both for
deposits and for loans principally by Manx people, whereas later collapses
affected Manx people to a much lesser degree, and then only as
depositors. Much has been written about the collapse of Dumbell's, but
perhaps the chief cause of the disaster was the speculation which
characterised the twelve years leading up to the collapse; failure to
capitalize the breweries amalgamation dealt the final blow[12].

There had already been several instances of banks collapsing in the
Island (such as the Isle of Man Joint Stock Banking Company 1843, Isle
of Man Commercial Banking Company 1848, and Bank of Mona 1878).
However, the establishment of The Isle of Man Banking Company, later
to become The Isle of Man Bank Limited, in 1865, the first company to
be registered with limited liability in the Island, laid the foundations for
the period of banking stability in the Island which lasted from after
Dumbell's collapse until the 1980s.

The financial services that were provided in the Island up to 1970
resembled those available in provincial towns throughout Britain. Banks
offered local branch banking and lending. Other comparable financial
services were available with insurance agencies from the early 19th
century, with stock-broking, accounting and auditing services often being
provided by the same people or firms. For example, Frederick S. Jackson's
advertisement in Brown's Directory of 1881 indicates the wide range of
services offered:

> Stock and share Broker, Estate Agent and Arbitrator, Auditor,
> Public Accountant and Auditor to the Isle of Man Steampacket
> Company, Business done in English and Foreign Stocks and Shares.
> Public Companies' Accounts carefully Audited. Sales and Transfers
> of Real Property and Mortgages negotiated with Secrecy and
> Despatch. Fire, Life, Marine, and Accidental Insurances Effected.

All in all, this operation would have taxed the skills of modern
financial supervision to the limit, yet Mr Jackson's sole qualification for
offering this broad spectrum of services was experience. In 1936, the firm

was taken over and became R. L. Stott & Co.

Besides banking, other financial services were introduced to meet the normal commercial needs of the Island. In 1886, W. H. Walker & Co set up office as the Island's first firm of chartered accountants, to be followed gradually by others. Tower Insurance was established as a general insurer in the Island in 1928, and the Conister Trust was formed in 1935 to provide loan or hire purchase finance for consumer purchases; both these were set up as public companies with Manx shareholders. By 1957, when the Society of Incorporated Accountants amalgamated with the Institute of Chartered Accountants, there were 12 chartered and 16 incorporated accountants, and for them the pace of professional life was relatively leisurely.[13] Likewise, the number of Manx advocates was small, and they were little involved with financial services. By 1982, there were only 28 practising advocates, compared with 141 qualified accountants[14] showing that at that stage most of the professional support for novel financial services was being provided by accountants.

Outside tourism the traditional Manx industries had been showing a steady decline. The last mine in Laxey closed in 1929, and the Manx fishing industry, already in decline, continued to contract. Agriculture too was in difficulties, and there was little manufacturing. Two World Wars interrupted the profitable visiting industry on which the Island's economy increasingly depended, although 'enemy alien' internment camps and military activity provided all-year employment and a market for local produce during these periods. In the First World War the Island accommodated as many as 24,500 internees. In the Second World War full use was made of the Island's tourist accommodation for internees, military bases and training camps. In addition, many Manxmen joined the forces. But even at its height, the visiting trade was seasonal, and, outside of wartime, work schemes in forestry and road building were devised to provide winter employment for Islanders, while others sought employment off-Island, such as lifting sugar beet in Norfolk.

At the end of the Second World War the Island looked to a resumption of normal pre-war life. For a time this seemed likely, but in the event things were to prove less simple.

CHAPTER 3

POST-WAR GLOOM

When the Second World War ended, the expectation in the Island was that the situation would return to pre-war patterns as had been the case after the Great War. Superficially, as far as tourism was concerned, things did revert to normal, with over 600,000 arrivals in 1947, 1948 and 1949, but this revival was not to last. Within a few years a gradual decline set in, although this did not give cause for immediate alarm. Indeed, in many quarters there was a refusal to accept that the old family mass summer holiday was a thing of the past. There was still a view that, with the appropriate investment and effort, the Island's economic future would largely depend on tourism.

This attitude should be viewed in the context of the political and economic situation of the United Kingdom. In May 1945, after the victory in Europe, the British electorate turned its back on Churchill and the Conservative party and elected a Labour government, which, for the first time in the party's history, obtained a substantial majority. The new government faced a difficult situation. The war had to a degree exhausted both the country's people and its economic resources. Much rebuilding, both physical and economic, was called for. The euphoria of victory was soon replaced by a pervading sense of gloom and the perception that life was becoming harder, not easier. In these unpromising circumstances, the government embarked on a programme of socialist purity that exacerbated the economic situation.

Despite the modern myth that Attlee's government was one of the greatest of 20th century and Attlee himself one of the greatest prime ministers, this was certainly not the feeling at the time. With the possible exception of the Prime Minister and the Foreign Secretary, Ernest Bevin, many of the Cabinet were clearly incompetent; the government lurched from crisis to crisis. In particular the economy, presided over by Sir Stafford Cripps, and undermined by nationalization, increased government expenditure and union unrest, was in serious difficulties. The culmination was the humiliating devaluation of the pound from four to 2.8 dollars to the pound. Foreign exchange for travel abroad was subject to strict control, with a limit of £50 per person. Food was in short supply; rationing was worse than during the war and now extended to bread and potatoes. There was a brief attempt in 1950 to de-ration sweets, but the resultant demand caused them to be re-rationed swiftly; the Labour party laughed to scorn the Conservative's election promise to dismantle all food rationing (which, after re-election in 1951, the party actually achieved). All of these factors were to affect the Isle of Man and its tourist trade.

Britain's economic problems were aggravated by a programme of nationalization of the 'Commanding Heights of the Economy' in accordance with good socialist doctrine. These 'Heights' included all utilities (electricity, gas, water, railways, buses, passenger shipping, airlines, ports) and primary commodities, coal and steel, with more nationalization promised in future governments. These promises featured in the famous Clause 4 of the Labour party manifesto, which has only been dropped comparatively recently. As if that were not enough, the government undertook a massive programme of social reform committing vast permanent government expenditure, firstly, by establishing a National Health service through the nationalisation of the trust hospitals and giving free health care to all; and secondly by introducing social security benefits comprising pensions and sickness and unemployment payments, paid for initially by National Insurance contributions. The government also extended the commitment to education, placing schools under local education authorities, raising the school leaving age, and extending state assistance for university education by means of State and County Major Scholarships.

The Isle of Man decided to adopt the health and social security reforms virtually in their entirety, and to make the benefits reciprocal and transferable in relation to the United Kingdom. Perhaps the Methodist heritage and instincts of many Manx, together with a strong sense of egalitarianism amongst a people which had never had an aristocracy or conspicuous wealth of its own, inclined them to follow the lead of the

Sir John Bolton.

Attlee government. Indeed, it might be argued that in these respects, the public policy and instincts of the Island are still close to those of Attlee's government. But, in following the lead of the United Kingdom, the Island's government took on the financial burdens of national health and social security, at the risk of bringing about, at some future time, government insolvency.

Tourism

The strong, if temporary post-war recovery of tourism to the Island from Britain may be ascribed to a variety of reasons. Before the war, relatively few British people had travelled to the Continent, let alone beyond. Although during the war many more Britons, especially servicemen, had travelled widely, they were perhaps not yet in the mood for further foreign adventures. Furthermore, although most people had limited means, the £50 spending money per person was a very small amount, even in those days. The same reasons that had attracted visitors to the Island a hundred years before still applied; the Island was exotic and entertaining; moreover, the £50 limit did not apply, and there seemed to be better food and more of it in the Island, where rationing was not quite so severe.

For a few years there seemed little cause for concern, with arrival numbers rising steadily to almost 625,000 in 1948, but soon afterwards the trend turned downwards, and by 1958 the arrivals had fallen to 447,000. This fall had begun to cause anxiety, and, in 1955 a Visiting Industry Commission was established under the chairmanship of J. W. Birch who was also commissioned by the Manx Government to undertake a study of the Island's economy. This study was finally published in 1964. The conclusion of these studies and commissions was that tourism was of vital importance to the Island's economy, and that, although the Government should make efforts to boost agriculture and fishing, and to attract more manufacturing, it should devote substantial financial resources to bringing tourist accommodation and attractions up to modern standards in order to reverse the decline and achieve arrivals figures in excess of one million. Birch concluded that:

> ...the favourable conditions in which the tourist industry developed to its peak prior to the First World War have changed substantially, and that in consequence the Island has suffered a weakening of its competitive position. Nevertheless, at an approximation, tourism is currently responsible for 75% of the Island's income from external sources, other than investments, and for as much as 60% of the gross value of the production achieved by those forms of industry that have been discussed... The extent of the Island's commitment to this specialized form of industry presents certain economic and social disadvantages, among which winter unemployment is generally accepted as being the most significant. In a serious form, such unemployment is, however, largely the product of a lack of any substantial investment in the improvement of the capital equipment

Clifford Irving.

of tourism during the off-season period; and, given a suitable programme of redevelopment, it would recede... The ... tourist industry is the Isle of Man's greatest asset in earning its living in a fiercely competitive world; ... all possible steps should be taken to rebuild and extend this industry and to give it every assistance available from modern techniques of publicity.[15]

The conclusion is remarkable, even for the time; it implies that throwing Government resources at the problem would be sufficient to counteract the overwhelming attraction of package tours by air to foreign destinations offering modern accommodation and guaranteed good weather. But, in the longer term, none of these proposals to spend large

Sir Ronald Garvey.

sums on tourism could achieve more than a delay of the inevitable decline. Clearly, some new strategy was called for.

Manufacturing

Successive Governments had encouraged the growth of manufacturing in the Island. Some of the enterprises produced products designed for the home market, such as milling, baking, brewing, and the manufacture of textiles, knitting and carpets. In the 1950s, special efforts were made to attract manufacturing for export off the Island with a number of incentives which included making available land, buildings, and grants in addition to low taxation. The manufacturing sector provided employment which, unlike agriculture and tourism, was not subject to seasonal fluctuation. The two most significant employers were the Ronaldsway Aircraft Company and Castletown Thermostats, later called 'Strix'. The Ronaldsway Aircraft Company, which made components for the Martin Baker Ejector Seats, came to the Island in 1952 and started production in 1954. Strix set up in 1951, initially in Bridge House, Castletown, later moving to the Cosy Cinema, and manufactured thermostat switches for electric kettles and blankets, based on an invention by John Taylor, an old boy of King William's College, the Island's public school.

Other manufacturers at this time included Dowty Engineering, Aristoc Stockings, Vulfix Brushes and the Ronaldsway Shoe Company. Manufacturing provided 14% of the Island's employment compared to 21% for tourism, which was responsible, according to Birch, for 75% of the Island's external income and 60% of economic output.[16]

The Manx Economy: Customs and Excise and Taxation

Despite all these initiatives, the Island's economy continued to decline; this is seen most dramatically in the drop in the Island's population figures from 55,253 in 1951 to 48,135 in 1961, the lowest since 1841[17]. There is no doubt that, in 1960, the general appearance of the Island was neglected and run down. Property was generally poorly maintained, and in 1960 only one new residence was started; almost every local builder put in for the work, but by the time of its completion in 1961, the building trade had begun to revive as people began to move to the Island, attracted by the low taxes on income. There is some statistical confirmation of this trend in the Douglas rating lists, where in both 1959 and 1960 there was a net decline of one household, but in 1961 an increase of 17.

From the total revenues of £3.5m of 1958/59, over the next three years revenues rose some 10% to £3.9m; but by 1965/66 to £5.3m and 1970/71 to £9.5m, of which income taxes now represented 38.5%.[18] This increase reflects the results of the abolition of surtax and the attraction of new residents.

Sir Charles Kerruish.

Constitutional Changes

Until 1958 the Island's power to take independent initiatives was limited, but during the governorship of Sir Ambrose Dundas (1952-1959) there were constitutional changes in the relationship between the Island and the British Government, as fundamental as those which had occurred under Governor Loch in 1866.

Firstly, under the Customs Agreement of 1957, the Island agreed to continue to keep all indirect taxes other than those on beer (customs, excise on tobacco, spirits, wines, fuel oils, etc., and purchase tax) at the same levels as in Britain, and to continue the Common Purse Arrangement. (The Common Purse Arrangement was the result of negotiations which had been conducted in 1894 between the Island authorities and the British Treasury in an effort to simplify the procedure of collecting Manx customs duties. Under this arrangement, duties on goods destined for the Island are collected on behalf of the British customs authorities, and assigned proportionately).

More importantly, the Isle of Man Act of 1958, together with the enactments of Tynwald, effectively removed the British Treasury's control of the Island's finances. Instead of the Lieutenant Governor effectively acting as agent of the UK government in financial matters, now, with the Lieutenant Governor's approval, Tynwald controlled the Island's revenue and expenditure.

This represented a major devolution of power from the British Treasury to the Governor within Tynwald, although the actual initiative still lay with the Governor as Chancellor of the Exchequer and Chief Executive, rather than with Tynwald itself. However, successive Governors did consult members of Tynwald in their formulation of policy. Sir Ambrose Dundas set up an Income Tax Commission in 1956, with four members of Tynwald and three tax experts, to examine policy on direct taxation.

The Abolition of Surtax

The main outcome of this Commission was the proposal, made in 1960 in the first budget speech of Dundas's successor, Sir Ronald Garvey (1959-66), that surtax should be abolished in the Island with the express aim of attracting new residents to boost the economy. The argument was that a resident would be present for 52 weeks in any year, in contrast to the fortnight spent in the Island by the average visitor, and would buy goods in the Manx shops, employ workers in the building trades to build, renovate or maintain housing stock, and also contribute to direct taxation on their incomes. It was suggested that every new resident would provide one new job.

The question has often arisen as to who first suggested this change which was to prove of such fundamental importance for the future of the Island. As a member of the Income Tax Commission, Clifford Irving, MHK for North Douglas, was certainly a party to the proposal; at the time, it was widely believed that the abolition of surtax was the achievement of John Bolton, MHK for North Douglas, who drove the legislation through Tynwald. His knighthood, bestowed in 1977, was generally assumed to reflect this contribution in particular, as well as his long service to Manx politics. But it is certain that Garvey, who embraced this crucial development and was to prove enthusiastic in promoting the interests of the Island even in the face of misgivings on the part of his Whitehall masters, played an important role. It would therefore appear reasonable to credit all three men acting in unison in the interests of the Island.

Although at the time there was some passing mention of the radical shift in taxation policy as providing a basis for banking and investment funds of a type newly introduced into Jersey, the whole purpose of the change, as presented to Tynwald, was to attract new residents to contribute to the Island's economy. Prior to the change, Manx surtax had been imposed at graduated rates up to 7/6d in the pound and had affected a relatively small number of high incomes (309). The standard rate of income tax was 22.5%, and surtax, paid in addition to income tax on incomes in excess of £2,500, was charged on a progressive ten-point scale ranging from 3.75% to 37.5%. The following year, the standard rate of income tax was reduced to 21.25% and from April 1961 no surtax on personal incomes was levied in the Isle of Man. Over the same period income and surtax rates in the United Kingdom rose to 7/9d income tax plus 10/- surtax, a total of 88.75%. In the UK, surtax was imposed at the full rate on comparatively low-level incomes. In 1960, furthermore, the prospect of a Labour Government winning the next general election, scheduled for 1964 at the latest, posed the threat of a probable return to confiscatory levels of taxation, making the Isle of Man even more attractive.

When, on 21 June 1960, Governor Garvey presented his budget proposing the abolition of surtax in the Island it was apparent that the loss of surtax would reduce the Island's revenues of some £3.9m by £35,000. The fact was that indirect taxes were hugely important to the Island as 65% of the Island's total revenue came from that source. Approximately half, £1.8m, was derived from customs and excise duties,

predominately on tobacco, with a further £500,000 from purchase tax.
Only £800,000 came from income tax. This explains why, despite the
tightness of the Government's funding, the risk involved in the loss of
£35,000 as a result of abolishing surtax was comparatively small. The
Governor's proposal was intended to achieve the first of three priorities
which he set out, that of attracting new permanent residents to the Island.
His second priority was to develop the tourist industry and the third was
to encourage the development of light industry. As an aside Garvey also
introduced the idea of issuing Isle of Man bank notes. It was therefore
hoped that the abolition of surtax, which would have a relatively small
effect on the Island's income, would in the long run have a
disproportionate benefit to the Island's economy.

Nevertheless, in certain quarters of Tynwald, for various reasons, the
proposal provoked strong reactions, the most rational of which can be
attributed to old-fashioned Socialism. Charles Kerruish, MHK for Garff,
though a member of the Government's Executive Council, was the first
to attack the proposal; he suggested a number of relatively minor ways in
which money could be spent on strategies intended to boost the Manx
economy, in the areas of agriculture, tourism and manufacturing. In
characteristically disparaging terms he commented:

> May I say, therefore, how much I regret the fact that you have rushed
> in to commend in your statement the vapourings of those I would
> term - with one exception - your woolly-minded advisers on the
> Income Tax Commission who hold up their hands in holy horror at
> personal gambling, but are prepared to gamble £85,000 [*sic*, for
> some reason the figure changed in the debate from £35,000 to
> £85,000] annually of public money on the faint chance of bringing
> the bigger and better tax dodgers here, while at the same time
> conceding to an already privileged section of our Island benefits
> which will inevitably be borne by their less privileged fellows. We
> must remember, as indeed you have recorded in your statement, sir,
> the godsend of the Welfare State as we know it. Those services -
> both health and social - which are non-existent in the Eldorados
> portrayed to us in certain reports as the example we must follow in
> the future. It is disheartening to find that you accept this form of

political spivvery in principle, while happily realising that it will
undoubtedly be spurned later in our debates. We, your Executive,
desire more constructive things from you.[19]

Edward Callister MLC, proceeded to dismiss the budget as 'anaemic',
lacking courage, imagination and initiative for the future.

Clifford Irving's response, 'as a woolly-minded member of the
Income Tax Commission' was that he felt 'exhausted after listening to the
honourable member for Garff [Kerruish] mounting and dismounting
from every political band wagon we can [have] had in the Isle of Man'.[20]

The discussion continued through the debate on the Income Tax
(No.2) Bill in November of 1960. The Bill was strongly recommended by
John Bolton, on the basis that, although it was an act of faith...'other
places which have abolished surtax [had] received very considerable
increases in the amount of income tax they [had] eventually collected'.
The proposal was strongly opposed by Jack Nivison, MHK for Onchan
(a leading contributor to Manx political development over a long period)
on the grounds of loss of revenue, which he estimated at £85,000. He
was not opposed to the rise of population to 75,000 or 100,000, but did
not believe that much tax would result from the new residents. He would
prefer to support a casino. 'We have not a favourable climate or other
favourable conditions to offer. In my view, this is a very dangerous
experiment'. Alf Teare, MHK for South Douglas, believed tourism and
new residents were linked, and that this was 'a time when many people
[were] coming from Africa and other places and [were] seeking places to
retire and settle down'. Howard Simcocks, an advocate and an MHK for
Rushen, believed that new residents would be predominantly people of
independent means who would contribute to the economy, and create
employment: '....if they [did] no more than provide jobs for our young
people so that they [did] not leave the Island, then they [would] have made
a valuable contribution'.

Much of the opposition to a Bill calculated to attract new residents
came from those who disliked what they saw as the social consequences
of the influx of wealthy outsiders; they claimed that money would be
better spent on tourism, manufacturing or straight handouts (but they

were unable to suggest how the revenue to produce such funds was to be generated). Albert Corkish, MHK for South Douglas, said that the money should be used to reduce the cost of living. Any spare money should be used to keep young people in the Island. Robert Stephen, a member of the Income Tax Commission, went against the Commission's own recommendations. He expressed the view that the 'Colonels and captains [had] one object - to maintain their position in retirement with little regard to the welfare of the Island'. William Quayle, MHK for Middle, said he did not think the principle behind this Bill was to 'encourage millionaires to come to the Island to reside'. He thought they wanted to encourage 'the middle income group, the people with, say, £2,000 a year, to come here'. Edward Callister remained wholly opposed; he believed that capital could be raised from the £7m invested by the Isle of Man Bank outside the Island. He did not 'want to rely on cleaning the shoes of the idle rich' and accused John Bolton of having a pecuniary interest in the proposal, along with the other 309 surtax payers.

Key to the whole debate was the notion of the new residents whom the abolition of surtax might attract; those who opposed the proposal were obsessed with the inevitability of its failure[21] but at the same time anxious about the consequences if it should succeed to attract rich immigrants whose behaviour might have a negative impact on the Island community. The Island's past experience of half-pay officers proved that these fears were not groundless.

George Gale, MHK for Peel, spoke of 'people from Poona...colonels and so on.... we are supposed to sell our birthright for a mess of pottage, and invite anyone to come to this Island without paying his due taxation'. Cecil McFee, MHK for Rushen, did not agree with the principle of 'attracting to the Isle of Man the idle rich'.

In this debate, only Hubert Radcliffe, MHK for Ayre, made reference to financial services: 'When England was at the height of its glory it was importing more than it exported. How then did it attain such heights? Because of invisible exports. We all know about them, those who study the subject, and we have invisible exports such as banking, shipping and insurance facilities and the investment of money...'. This appears to have been the only official reference to such financial services.

In this debate, many members of the House of Keys displayed an inability to understand economic realities, reacting emotionally rather than rationally, a failing that may still be observed in many cases today.

Clifford Irving, as seconder, now spoke in favour of the Income Tax Bill, although somewhat equivocally. The proposal was passed at second reading by fifteen votes to nine in the Keys and seven votes to one in the Legislative Council, to take effect from 6th April 1961.

And so the scene was set, and the Island awaited the consequences which, in the event, proved to be much more radical than was apparent during the Tynwald debates.

CHAPTER 4

ARRIVALS

New Residents

And so again new people began to come to the Island. But what attracted them, and which areas of the Island did they come to? What effect did the influx of newcomers have?

In the event, the increase in the number of new residents arriving on the Island was gradual; by 1966 the population had grown by only 1,179. The total figure was still less than 50,000. By 1971, however, the overall population had increased by 5,269, and each of the subsequent five-year census figures indicated an average growth of some 1,200 per annum. After 1981, however, the picture was to change. In the years that followed, population figures virtually stagnated, until 1987. In between censuses it is more difficult to discover actual numbers, since people from other parts of the British Isles are free to take up residence in the Island without formality, unless they wish to enter employment, when a work permit will normally be required.[22]

At one time, the Island was known to comparatively few people outside the North of England. Even for those who knew its precise location (and did not confuse it with the Isle of Wight), the image its name conjured up was that of a bleak wind-swept northern seaside resort, inevitably linked with the TT races and with old music hall songs such as *Kelly From The Isle of Man*. Many newcomers were expecting to find some poor relation of the Channel Islands (they found themselves somewhat taken aback by the reality). So what motivated them to move to the Island in the first place, apart from the attractive low taxation and the ability to bring their capital intact?

One important factor was that there were fewer obstacles to moving to the Isle of Man than to the Channel Islands. Firstly, the perception was that Jersey in particular welcomed only super-rich 'celebrity' incomers.

The Channel Islands operated an elaborate system of residency, with qualifications in various categories depending on such factors as birthright, employers' staffing requirements, and straight wealth and tax contributions to the Jersey treasury. Even the actor John Nettles, who was starring in the Jersey detective series *Bergerac* encountered problems when he wished to take up residence there. House prices, too, were very high in Jersey and neighbouring Guernsey. Guernsey controlled immigration through open and closed housing lists, the closed lists being reserved for those who can claim Guernsey family connexions.

There was, moreover, a lack of space for newcomers in the Channel Islands. The islands are small, about one eighth and one twelfth respectively of the area of the Isle of Man, yet Jersey's population exceeds that of Man, while that of Guernsey is not much smaller.[23] Those wishing to move to different jurisdictions for tax purposes, especially those from the North West of England who already knew something of the Isle of Man, turned their eyes towards the Island where housing was plentiful and cheap, even if much of the housing stock was in need of improvement, where there was ample space and where newcomers could take up residence with minimal formality.

There was another factor which helped to make the Island an attractive location. The 1960s was the period which marked the end of Empire, consequently many professional people, lawyers, doctors, and accountants, as well as colonial administrators and police and colonial settlers, sometimes families who had lived abroad for several generations, were looking to return to Britain. Over time their family and social ties to Britain had become attenuated or had been severed altogether so settling there was not an imperative. Moving to the Isle of Man, however, was very attractive; it offered these people many advantages. It was British, and thus reassuringly familiar, but at the same time they were protected from the high rates of UK taxation.

Few incomers, except for returning Manx people, came to the Island from India - curiously enough in view of the pointed remarks about 'Colonels from Poona' during the Tynwald debate on the abolition of surtax. Rather the majority came from the Caribbean or Africa. Incomers from the Caribbean, largely from Jamaica and Trinidad, included, amongst others, Sir Kenneth Blackburn, the Governor General of the abortive West Indies Federation. These newcomers settled in easily, perhaps being more accustomed to island life. However, many who came from Africa retained their old Colonial ways, sometimes referring to the Manx as 'natives'. These new residents were often heard lamenting times past and how life was in colonial times and consequently they became known as 'When-Is' (as in 'When I was in Bulawayo'). Many stories circulated the Island concerning the *bons mots* of the When-Is such as the occasion two of them were overheard lamenting their misfortune because a 'native' (in fact, a Manx advocate) had bought a house between their two properties in Maughold. On another occasion, a woman attending a dinner party given by Manx people with other Manx present broke off from her diatribe against the Manx, exclaiming: 'Oh dear, I am speaking in the presence of natives'; the vivid riposte of one of the Manx ladies present cannot be here repeated.[24]

Other 'come-overs' moved to the Island from England and Ireland. Those from the north of England took up residence in many parts of the Island and although their manner was often brash they found the place familiar, if rather sleepy, with a slower pace of life than that to which they had been accustomed. In many cases their families had known the Island for generations as many Manx families had their own, often comparatively recent, origins in the north of England, especially Lancashire.

Many of these incomers brought or started businesses in the Island; the entrepreneurs included the founders of Kwik Save, Ken Nicholson and Albert Gubay. In 1971 Nicholson started a cut-price store on the old holiday camp site in Victoria Road in Douglas, which, as Shoprite, not only undercut the prices of existing local shops but in many cases offered an improvement in quality. The business has been continued since Nicholson's death by his sons. Albert Gubay, who, along with his numerous enterprises elsewhere went on to found the Celtic Bank, redeveloped the Clinch's Brewery site on Douglas North Quay, and developed a new hotel at Mount Murray on the outskirts of Douglas. There were other businessmen attracted to the Island as well. The

Fern Cottage, the Howe. This cottage was insensitively modernized in 1960s, and quite disproportionally extended in the 1980s; an interesting contrast to the cottage next door (see opposite).

Horsthuis family, from Holland, came to start a wholesale greengrocer's business under the name of Robinson's in 1975, using retail outlets which included the Shoprite stores; the Harper family from Lancashire, who had for many years spent holidays in the Island, now established themselves permanently in the Isle of Man: the four members of the younger generation have practised as accountants and an advocate in the Island for many years.

But many of the wealthier incomers who came in many cases from the South of England, and the Anglo-Irish, the Ascendancy from the Irish Republic, tended, like the incomers from Africa, to huddle together. Many of them settled in or around Ramsey in the north of the Island, creating their own somewhat clannish community, rather as the half-pay officers had done in a previous age. This exclusivity and apparent sense of superiority was perceived by some locals as provocation, and the wealthy new residents became the targets of satirical criticism and hostility from the nascent Manx nationalist movement. The most conspicuous case was

Lhergy Cottage, the Howe. This cottage was well restored and sympathetically extended for modern living in the 1970s, keeping a thatched roof.

that of Mimi, Marchioness of Queensbury, who owned a large bungalow at Llergydhoo, north of Peel. When it was rumoured that she was proposing to close off a long-used footpath to the beach in 1973, her house was daubed with the slogan 'Tax Dodgers Get Out'.

There is no doubt that almost immediately after the abolition of surtax the Island experienced a building boom. The casual observer might also have noted the improvement in the appearance of the Island's existing buildings: new coats of paint were applied, derelict or dilapidated housing was converted, extended and modernised and as the 1970s approached it became more difficult for would-be purchasers to find properties suitable for renovation, and so the construction of a succession of purpose-built estates was undertaken. Smaller houses, mostly bungalows, were also being built in north Ramsey and on the outskirts of Port Erin. The Booilushag estate, which comprised more spacious bungalows on large plots of land, was erected south of Maughold at Port Mooar, a stretch of beautiful and previously unspoilt coastline. It is hard to imagine that such a development would have received planning permission at a later date. Another large estate was developed at Ballakillowy, outside Port Erin. Doubtless these spacious bungalows provide agreeable residences, offering spectacular views, but it cannot be claimed that they have contributed any architectural distinction to the Island landscape. Indeed, the Island offers a wealth of spectacular views, but there is no doubt that its principal attraction for incomers has been the protection from taxation.

Residence and Domicile

There were various ways in which the Island's tax regime was attractive to incomers, and to understand the advantages, would-be new residents had to be familiar with the concepts of *domicile* and *residence* in English and Manx law. Domicile and residence are two separate and distinct concepts as an individual may well be resident in one country but domiciled in another.

Residence is the simpler of the two: it involves physical presence within a taxing jurisdiction and, often more importantly, physical absence, particularly from the UK, sometimes taken together with the availability of accommodation. For the purposes of the UK, a person who is present for over six months in any year of assessment (6 April to 5 April of the following year) or for more than three months per year over a period of four consecutive years, is regarded as resident. Persons who are, for tax purposes, classed as resident in the UK are, unless protected by a non UK domicile, liable for UK income tax and capital gains tax on all income and gains from whatever source.

Domicile is distinct from nationality or residence. It is the concept of a permanent place of belonging, the home to which, even when absent, the individual intends to return; the acquisition of domicile may be a function of birth or of choice, and, if of choice, must be supported by a way of life and behaviour which demonstrate that the person really belongs to that new place. There are various well known tests of domicile (grave plots, bank accounts, etc.,) that may or may not be relevant, but it is usually possible to establish a domicile of choice by proper planning and pattern of life. There is also a transitional stage of 'deemed domicile' in

Scarlett House. An old Manx farmhouse, given a smart new front in the 18th century, well restored and preserving its forecourt.

the UK for those who have lived there for seventeen out of the last twenty years. 'Deemed domicile' is relevant for capital transfer and inheritance tax.

In order to enjoy the full fiscal benefits of moving outside the UK an individual needed to rearrange his life in accordance with these concepts of residence and domicile.

Returning Manx people and those who had lived for years outside the UK, in Africa, the Irish Republic or the Caribbean, were able to establish a Manx domicile with comparative ease. For those moving in from the UK the situation was less straightforward; proper planning was called for. The rewards of a Manx residence and domicile could, and still can, be substantial in terms of tax saved. With proper advice and tax planning a person moving successfully to the Isle of Man can avoid UK income tax (except on income generated in the UK from pensions, interest and dividends), capital gains tax, and capital transfer tax. Furthermore, once Manx domicile is successfully established a person may, with careful planning and due caution, exceed the permitted number of days in the UK without exposing all his income to UK. It is by carefully using this situation that many rich foreigners have been able to live permanently in the UK virtually free of UK tax (although the 2008 budget introduced a £30,000 tax charge for those that wish to continue to enjoy this privilege).

In 1964 and again in 1966 the Labour Party with Harold Wilson as Prime Minister won a majority in the House of Commons for their socialist agenda. Once again there followed the mismanagement of the economy, this time under Jim Callaghan as Chancellor of the Exchequer. This led to the 1967 financial crisis and the devaluation of the pound, despite the Government slogan 'the pound in your pocket will be just as valuable'. Roy Jenkins took over as Chancellor and stabilized the pound and, to a degree, the economy, but this was only achieved by high rates of taxation. Labour introduced two new taxes, as well as changing the old income tax and surtax into corporation tax for companies and a combined income tax and surtax for individuals rising in steps to 98%. After the financial crisis of 1967 a further 5% was temporarily added to the top, bringing taxation to 103% of every additional pound of income. These levels of taxation not only invited legal avoidance through such measures as moving outside the jurisdiction, but also illegal evasion. In 1965, in order to claw back all possible gains, the government had also introduced the highly unpopular Capital Gains Tax. If assets such as property, shares, even pictures and furniture, were sold for a higher return than their 1965 value, then this profit was taxed, and initally no allowance was made for inflation.

On Labour's return to government in 1974 they continued tightening their tax regime. The following year Estate Duty, which could be avoided by lifetime gifts, was abolished in favour of Capital Transfer Tax, which could not. However, both could be avoided by moving to the Isle of Man and becoming resident and in due course domiciled.

Knock Rushen House. This house, not far from Scarlett House, was, until 1986, similar to it, with a
pretty façade and texture, and a most attractive forecourt. The five righthand bays were the original.
The insensitive extensions have destroyed its external attractive proportions, texture and setting.
An example of how not to modernize or convert.

An example of the type of new residents attracted to the Island at this
time is that of Peter and Stella Thrower, an Australian couple who had for
many years worked in the University and the Chinese University of Hong
Kong. In 1973, they happened to see an advertisement by the Isle of Man
Bank in the paper Sunday Business, which had been wrapping some
vegetables they had bought from an itinerant trader in Hong Kong, which
read as follows:

The Isle of Man - A tax haven in the British Isles

The Isle of Man is part of the British Isles; but it is not part of the
UK for the purposes of taxation. As such it offers distinct financial
advantages: it has a low income tax and the Isle of Man
Government imposes no Surtax, no Estate Duties, and no Capital
Gains Tax.

The advertisement invited interested parties to address enquiries to the Isle of Man Bank; this the Throwers duly did, opening an account with the bank. In 1974 they acquired a cottage in the Island and upon retirement in 1985 they moved over permanently. They had at one point also considered retiring to the Channel Islands, but were put off by what they saw as the locals' attitude to new arrivals, and by the lack of a National Health Service.

Immigration Control

Although population growth in the Island had been gradual since 1961, by 1970 the pace of immigration was increasing; most new residents were not here to work. The consequent demand for housing not only caused a building boom in the Island, but also forced up the price of properties. Despite the benefits to the Island's economy in respect of taxation revenue and money spent on buildings, shops, restaurants, etc., a noticeable group of Manx people were moved to express their disapproval through the new nationalist movement *Fo Halloo* (Manx Gaelic for 'Underground'). *Fo Halloo* reviled and mocked Manx politicians, especially John Bolton, MLC, and financiers, particularly R. T. D. Stott; but their principal target was one Judah Binstock,[25] a solicitor who was not actually resident on the Island. Binstock, astutely foreseeing the pressing demand for building land, had taken out options on, or purchased speculatively, extensive areas of farmland around the outskirts of Douglas and Onchan, correctly assuming that in due course it would be needed for expansion. Smaller investors, too, sought to benefit by property speculation. How many Manx people owe the meteoric rise in their fortunes to similar successful property speculation is a matter for conjecture.

Inevitably, the need to react quickly to the developing situation caught politicians on the back foot. Perhaps the most interesting reaction was that of Clifford Irving, who, at the March sitting of Tynwald of 1973, called for the 'severe restriction' of new residents. As Chairman of the Tourist Board he had been charged with the job of advertising for new residents, but had not actually done so for two years. In an interview with

Scarlett Road, Castletown. A bungalow development along the Castletown shore. It is saved from complete barbarity only by the pre-existing coastal wall. The subsequent motley extensions probably improve the appearance.

the *Manx Star*,[26] he stated that the influx of new residents over the past 12 years had changed a situation of over 1,000 unemployed and a loss of 700 a year in population, to the present full employment and a fair degree of prosperity. Government revenue had increased enormously; without the tax contributions of its wealthy retired new residents and new industrialists, the Island would be unable to maintain its social, health and education services at their present level.

However, he conceded that unrestricted immigration put a strain on health and social services and also had a detrimental effect on the landscape, on housing prices, and quality of life. Without wishing to upset what he called 'the new Manx', who, he claimed, were often well-assimilated and eager to preserve the Manx way of life, he stressed the necessity for immigration controls, on a par with those in operation elsewhere. He favoured granting residence only to those who had some connection with the Island, or those who could make a reasonable contribution to its economy - i.e., economically active, and wealthy retired people paying a substantial amount of tax.

While deploring the posting of offensive signs such as 'English Pigs Go Home' by extremists, he claimed he did not object to the 'extremists' conducting a decent propaganda campaign. 'At least they counterbalance the extremists at the other end of the scale - the Manx Mafia,' he concluded gnomically. (It remains somewhat of a mystery to whom the expression referred, although the same expression was still being used in the 1980s, by David Cannan, MHK for Michael, with a knowing look. Possibly it was a derogatory reference to those Manx professionals, based largely in Athol Street, the Island's hub of finance, who appeared to be doing rather too well out of the circumstances of the 1970s, together with persons of influence inside and outside politics).

Clifford Irving said he did not believe that the present housing difficulties experienced by young Manx people were attributable solely to the Island's New Residents policy, but he admitted that home ownership, despite Government support, was now beyond the reach of many of the Island's young people. The Government and local authorities needed to build many more rental properties.

He had been most impressed, he said, by the fact that it was not now just an extreme minority which opposed the New Residents policy; there was widespread opposition amongst moderates as well. The Island would always need new residents, but selectivity was needed to ensure that the Island's special quality of life was not 'swamped out of existence'. For this reason, restrictions must be imposed before it was too late. It is interesting to note that this was the position of that same Clifford Irving who was to claim the credit for the successful consequences, in terms of increased revenue and higher population figures, which resulted from the abolition of surtax.

There was certainly a sense that something needed to be done and so, in 1974, despite some misgivings on the part of Bill Dawson, the Island's Treasurer, a Land Speculation Tax was introduced, aimed at taxing high profits on property deals. The new tax was imposed at 21½ pence, the income tax rate, and this despite that fact that Section 2(1)(a) and (b) of the comparatively recent Income Tax Act of 1970 had already made provision for taxing such gains, had the Assessor but shown the courage

Typical bungalow developments of the 1970s in north Ramsey. Port Erin suffered similarly.

to use the provision of the Act and raise the appropriate assessment.

Nationalists and politicians alike hoped to tax (punitively rather than in the interests of increasing revenue) the gains made by profiteers and speculators, but the new legislation did not prove an efficient instrument for their purpose; besides, it also affected people who had never set out to make a profit, but were simply benefiting from rising prices. In 1985, when property prices were falling, the Land Speculation Tax was finally abolished, having achieved little of its intended purpose, hardly deterring speculators, but interfering with the operation of the housing market.

Between 1981 and 1986, there was little change in the Island's
population figures, and property prices stagnated. But the announcement
by Jersey and Guernsey in March 1987 that both these islands were
restricting the number of new businesses and business employees
triggered a new population explosion in the Isle of Man, even though
those governments removed the restrictions shortly afterwards when they
saw how many of their businesses were setting up alternative offices in
the Isle of Man. The Government proclaimed that this was a more
beneficial immigration, comprising economically active employees,
primarily in the finance sector. However, the influx provoked a resurgence
of nationalism. The new extremists, who called themselves *FSFO*, were,
perhaps, less colourful than *Fo Halloo* and did not produce regular
publications, but their protests, like those of their predecessors,
occasionally took the form of acts of arson on residential building sites.

Tourism - and the Casino

During this period, in response to the will of Tynwald and of many
Manx people, tourism was not neglected. In accordance with the second
priority mentioned in Sir Ronald Garvey's budget speech of 21st June
1960, the sector was encouraged by the provision of grants and loans over
a ten-year period under the Hotel and Boarding House Improvement Act
and the Tourist Accommodation Improvement Act. Governor Garvey
also proposed the construction of a new port terminal building in
Douglas, a new swimming pool for Douglas, a new TT grandstand and
the extension of the runway at Ronaldsway Airport.

In practice, Government expenditure on tourist-sector projects was in
fact considerable. Such projects included the new sea terminal, opened by
Princess Margaret in July 1965, and an ambitious new concept in all-
weather entertainment, the Aquadrome and Summerland complex, which
opened on 9th July 1971 on the former Derby Castle site (though
tragically the complex was to burn down, with considerable loss of life on
2nd August 1973). In addition, the Government assumed responsibility
for the Gaiety Theatre, a Frank Matcham jewel on Douglas promenade,

Smiles from Mr. Casino

W. A. Albury from Baltimore receiving the casino concession from the Chairman of the Board of Control, J. M. Cain, MHK.

thereby saving it from demolition as proposed by Sir Dudley Cunliffe-Owen, Managing Director of the Palace Group which owned it. Amongst other conspicuous contributions to tourism was the large extension to the Castle Mona Hotel in 1962, and the establishment of a casino, the first in the British Isles, in the Castle Mona Hotel and subsequently in the Palace Hotel, which was built as a condition of the concession.

It was perhaps this founding of the casino and the arrival of the pirate Radio Caroline which brought the Island colourfully to wider notice, unfortunately dramatically augmented subsequently by the Summerland fire. The possibility of establishing a casino to encourage tourism throughout the year had first been raised back in the 1950s, and Garvey embraced the idea. The necessary legislation was passed in April 1962, and the operating concession was granted to a Mrs Saul, and two other Americans from Maryland who had been involved with casinos in America. As part of the concession they were required to build a new hotel and casino on part of the recently-acquired Palace theatre site, and to pay a percentage of their takings to the Isle of Man Government.

The early days of the casino were full of drama. The establishment was formally opened by the glamorous film star Diana Dors on 27th May 1963. Various 'high rollers', including the Governor of Nevada, regularly flew in from the United States and Canada to gamble, but not all of them honoured their debts. From the very outset the enterprise encountered problems. Notwithstanding, satisfactory accounts had to be presented to Government. Douglas Bolton, who was the auditor, recalls being threatened to sign accounts he believed to be inaccurate by having a pistol held to his head (despite the attempts at intimidation, Bolton refused). To make matters worse, it was discovered that not all the takings on which the levy to the Government was based were being recorded, and the Government, as well as Mrs Saul herself, or so she claimed, were being defrauded.

The Isle of Man Gaming Board's inspectors employed in the Casino gaming rooms reported to the Board's auditors, W H Walker & Co, whose senior partner was Alec Crowe, that they believed the conduct of certain staff should be investigated. The suspicion was that gaming room staff were inflating their records of winnings and retaining the difference, a process known as taking the 'cut off the top'. The senior inspector held highly secret discussions with Crowe late at night, either at 50 Athol Street or at Crowe's home. Crowe decided that undercover agents should be sent in. Members of Walker's staff were given cash to gamble with in the Casino and they were also provided with notebooks and stubby pencils short enough for them to make surreptitious notes in their coat pockets. They were to make a note of any winnings they had. The undercover operation was carried on for a week, at which point the police were consulted, and it was decided to mount a raid on the gaming rooms at 5am on Sunday, December 15th, 1963, just as they would be closing. The intention was to 'freeze' the night's records and seize the accounts that had been kept.[27]

The task force consisted of police officers, under the late Detective Sergeant George Turnbull, and W. H. Walker staff, led by Crowe. The Walker contingent included Jim Cain, later senior partner (and

Palace Hotel and Casino. Built in 1966 as part of the casino concession in the cheapest modern style to satisfy the conditions. The Falcon Cliff, seen above, built in 1882, once had a large dance hall attached. It has been converted successfully into offices. The flats beyond the hotel were built in two styles on the site of the Palace View and other boarding houses.

subsequently Speaker of the House of Keys), Neil Crowe, son of Alec Crowe, at the time a partner in the London office but who was back in the Island on holiday, and two future partners, Bob Cowin and Donald Newby.

The raiders held their rendez-vous in the early hours of the morning, in a quiet road off the seafront, well away from the Castle Mona. The police waited in their cars, the accountants in Crowe's car, with Neil Crowe at the wheel. (When he inadvertently sounded his horn as they waited in the dark, his accompanying policeman remarked 'Steady, lad!'). Shortly after 5am, they pounced. The raid went smoothly. Gaming room staff were isolated in different rooms, all the papers were seized, and Alec Crowe and Jim Cain set up a temporary office in a hotel cloakroom, where they spent the entire day questioning the staff, while, in the gaming rooms, the 'audit' went on.

The critical factor in the operation was accountancy, pure and simple, but the big breakthrough was the discovery of what came to be known as 'Pandora's Box', the cache of 'cut-off-the-top' money, concealed, according to the subsequent prosecution case in the courts, in a cupboard. When one of the Americans was asked to open the cupboard, the first object he brought out was a shotgun. There followed a moment of high tension, but the man simply laid the weapon aside. The scene was witnessed by Douglas Bolton, who was summoned during the night by Mrs Saul as her auditor, and by John Crellin, similarly summoned as her advocate - the latter, in the middle of a Territorial Army exercise, incongruously appearing in full uniform, thus adding to the surreal aspect of the scene.

Eventually, four Americans were brought to trial, charged with conspiracy to steal. They were convicted and sentenced to prison. However, their counsel, Rose Heilbron QC, took their case to appeal on the grounds that Deemster Moore's summing-up to the jury had been faulty. The appeal was upheld; the Americans went free, and the concession passed to a group associated with the well-known gaming club Crockfords of London, represented in the Island by Sir Dudley Cunliffe-Owen and Tim Holland. After later passing through the hands of Alan Fairley (formerly deputy chairman of Grand Metropolitan) in association with Judah Binstock and the Whipp family, it came under the control of Sir Douglas Clague's Palace Group in 1976. The Palace Group ran both the casino and the hotel until both passed into the control of Stakis, Ladbroke's and Gala in rapid succession, all far less colourful than their predecessors.

Apart from the casino, Government support for the tourist industry had met with some measure of success, but had failed to achieve the numbers required to sustain the Manx economy, despite claims during the surtax debate of 1960 that government expenditure on tourism would restore tourist numbers. To an increasing degree, arrival figures were made up of more than movements of residents and tourists. Increasing numbers of business people travelled to the Island, often for short periods, in connection with the finance sector. Between 1959 and 1978, arrivals numbers were generally between 400,000 and 500,000, occasionally more; but in 1979, the celebrations for the alleged millennium of the foundation of the Manx parliament, Tynwald, pushed

The site of the Queen's Hotel, Ramsey, which suffered a mysterious fire during which the owner and his canary had been taking a walk, has now been filled with apartments overlooking the bay and the Queen's Pier.

arrival figures up to 634,616, on a par with the boom years of 1913 and 1948. (There is little historical substantiation for the date of the foundation of Tynwald; the year 979 may well be too late; but the millennium celebrations in 1979 successfully raised the Island's profile worldwide, and the date has been generally accepted).[28]

In 1981, arrivals figures again fell below 500,000, and in the 1980s and 1990s, despite attempts to encourage tourism, they remained around the 300,000 mark. In recent times tourism attracts those people who enjoy wider cultural, sporting and scenic interests and generally spend more, having higher expectations regarding food and accommodation. By the late 1990s, even the most conservative Members of Tynwald had finally, after some forty years, faced reality and accepted that the Island's heyday as the Mecca of mass tourism was over. The hotels that lined the promenade were released to other uses; the almost unbroken sweep of Victorian façades stretching around Douglas bay was disrupted.

Manx Currency and other Ventures

During his Governorship of the Island, Sir Ronald Garvey's other ideas included the proposal that Manx Government bank notes should be issued, to replace both the notes issued by local banks and Bank of England notes. Not only would this promote the Island by raising public awareness, he suggested, but the amount of the note issue would in effect be an interest-free loan to the Government. The amount of the currency issued would be set aside and invested. This procedure has continued ever since. The first notes were issued on 6th July 1961, and the Island later gained much publicity when it retained the 10/- note after it was abolished in England, and again in the 1970s, when it issued virtually indestructible plastic notes, though it was soon discovered that, if heated in the oven, these turned into a miniature brick, perfect in all particulars. More unfortunately it became apparent that with use the notes became sticky and smelly and it was perhaps fortunate that in the 1980s the note manufacturers were no longer able to supply them. But the Treasury went on to pioneer an issue of a gold bullion coin as well as silver and platinum commemorative coins, and in July 1973 it took over the Island's Royal Mail, enabling Manx stamps to project the Island's image throughout the world.

Not all of Sir Ronald's ideas came to fruition. He believed that the Island would derive great benefit from the establishment of an oil refinery on 275 acres of the northern plain of the Ayres This would be owned by Natomas, an American company, but would be called IMP (Isle of Man Petroleums), and would process 10,000 barrels of oil a day. In 1965 Tynwald proposed a General Development Bill to enable this project, and others like it, to go ahead. In the face of the understandable outrage of environmentalists, the plan was finally abandoned in 1972.

In 1964 Garvey's enlightened Governorship also saw the

establishment of Radio Manx, formed by the Isle of Man Broadcasting Company on behalf of the Manx Government. This station had limited range but was able to broadcast to the Island its own news and programmes. More dramatically, on Tynwald Day of the same year, the shipboard pirate station Radio Caroline dropped anchor in Ramsey Bay. Here it was to remain, with the widespread approval of the Manx people and creating good publicity for the Island, until it was forced to close down by the British Government in March 1968.

Existing businesses expanded and new manufacturing ventures were encouraged, some of which were of an unusual nature such as the manufacture of the world's smallest car, the P5, in Peel in the 1960s. These initiatives formed part of the third priority set out in Garvey's 1960 budget speech.

There was also a number of colourful and controversial entrepreneurs who sought to introduce new and often inspired, ideas. One such, in the 1960s, was Manxman Bill Kerruish, grandson of 'Abdullah' Quilliam.[29] He was instrumental, inter alia, in the takeover of the Palace and Derby Castle company, enabling the Palace Hotel to be built on the one site and Summerland on the other, though not all of his enterprises were successful, and many people lost money. He was finally jailed for fraud.

Another ambitious businessman was Leslie Salts, who acquired the Mitre Hotel and other hotels in Ramsey and elsewhere, and promoted a scheme for the development of a yachting marina and shipyard in Ramsey harbour, doubtless with a view to suitably profitable development round the harbour basin. Salts arrived in the Island 1967, but by 1974 he was in serious financial difficulties. An Order of Arrest was issued against his assets by Deemster Eason.[30] It seemed that at that time the Isle of Man attracted these larger-than-life characters, not all of whom enhanced the reputation of the Island.

Other tourist enterprises foundered, including the Ramsey Hydro, now renamed the Grand Island Hotel, despite considerable government expenditure on its modernization. Various hands took an interest also in the Fort Anne Hotel, formerly a grand mansion overlooking Douglas harbour, once home to the founder of the RNLI, Sir William Hillary. In the end this building had become so dilapidated and unstable that demolition was the only option, leaving irrecoverable indebtedness of one million pounds with the Savings and Investment Bank, an institution that was to feature in a dramatic way in the 1980s. The Majestic Hotel in Douglas and the Bay Queen in Port St Mary were also in difficulty. The Golf Links Hotel in Derbyhaven was already obliged to close during the winter months, and in 1979 Mannington's five brewery hotels, including the Castle Mona, followed suit.[31]

Not all entrepreneurs were unsuccessful; notably, Sir Douglas Clague, returning from the Far East with substantial capital, acquired the Palace, the Golf Links, a substantial share of Heron and Brearley, and other assets. In general, however, reduced visitor numbers had led to a decline in the viability of tourist enterprises. The Island's general prospects for prosperity would have been gloomy indeed, had it not been for the beneficial consequences of the abolition of surtax, the contribution to the economy made by new residents, and the burgeoning financial services industry.

CHAPTER 5

FIRST STEPS IN FINANCE

The Early Years

The abolition of surtax, last paid in the Island in the tax year 1960/61, slowly began to attract new residents. However, apart from arrangements made specifically to accommodate the financial needs of the new arrivals, there were at first few moves towards introducing the provision of financial services specifically designed to take advantage of the Island's tax haven status for users outside the Island.

Before 1960 the Island had offered the type of financial services one might have expected to find in any English market town. Apart from the Midland Bank, which opened in the Island in 1965, the main English clearing banks already had an Island presence. Barclays Bank had opened a branch in Douglas in 1922. In 1969, Barclays merged with Martins Bank Limited, which had already established branches in Douglas, Castletown, Peel, Ramsey and Port Erin. Lloyds Bank had been present with three branches since 1900; Lloyds later took over the Trustee Savings Bank to become Lloyds TSB. Parr's Bank Limited had acquired the goodwill and premises of Dumbell's Banking Company Limited, amalgamating in 1918 with the London County & Westminster Bank Limited. In 1923 the name was changed to Westminster Bank Limited, and in 1970 the businesses of National Provincial Bank Limited, Westminster Bank Limited and District Bank Limited were merged in National Westminster Bank Limited. In 1961, the National Provincial Bank had taken over the Isle of Man Bank; with the exception of the Isle of Man Bank with its twelve branches, other banks continued to operate as branches of their UK principals, ignoring the potential advantages offered by the Island's offshore status until well into the 1980s.

There were two firms of stockbrokers, R. L. Stott & Co, which, under its former name, Jacksons, dated back to 1882, and Ramsey Crookall &

Athol Street, Douglas.
The famous street was built as a new residential development in the late Georgian
period, but by the 1860s some of them were being converted for professional use.
W. H. Walker & Co had their offices in number 50 by 1890.
The shadow is visible on both sides of the street.

Co, established in 1946, operating through London or provincial agents. The Tower Insurance Company had been founded with outside shareholders in 1928, but had been taken over by the Globe around 1946 as a precaution against nationalization by the Labour government in an early identification of the advantages of the Island's separate jurisdiction. The company asked the manager to identify a hundred houses in the Island for their key staff. Later, the Tower passed into the ownership of the Royal of Liverpool when it took over the Globe.

The number of advocates and accountants was limited to the figure required by a domestic market. When John Crellin was articled in 1956 he became one of 22 advocates, several of whom, including Barry Stanley and Bill Ashton, were working in England. Others, like Colin Fick who worked in Uganda, sought employment overseas because of a lack of opportunity in the Island. (Many Manx people in all sectors between the ages of 16 and 40 faced unemployment and had left the Island). Many advocates returned to the Island as activity increased in the 1960s; however, even by 1982, they numbered only 28.[32] John Crellin was admitted to the Manx Bar in 1956, and Martin Moore, after a law degree and calling to the English Bar, in 1963. It was to be some years before the next advocate was admitted to the Manx Bar.

Similarly, a dinner held in April 1954 in connection with the amalgamation of the Incorporated Society of Accountants with the Institute of Chartered Accountants was attended by twelve chartered and sixteen incorporated accountants, only seventeen of whom were in practice, and twenty students.[33] By 1970, there were 52 accountants in practice; by 1982, the number had risen to 141. Jim Cain[34] recollects that, when he returned to the Island in 1954 as a partner of the long-established firm of W. H. Walker & Co, it was clearly understood that he would be able to return to the Liverpool partnership if the work should prove insufficient for two resident partners. For these professionals, well into the 1960s, life proceeded at a much more leisurely pace than later.

But as the new residents began to arrive, although traditional banking services were adequate for their needs, there was more work for advocates, and in particular for accountants whose principal task concerned new residents' taxation. However, many incomers needed investment advice. Dursley Stott[35] recounts that many of those who had retired from the colonies held their capital in British government gilts, which were often, like War Loan, undated, and offered little protection for their retirement. In addition to individual investment portfolios, his firm identified a need for collective investments, particularly for smaller savings, to give balanced cover. With this in mind, Stott established three investment trusts for such investors in 1964, Manx and Overseas Investment Trust, Isle of Man and General Investment Trust, and Vannin

Victory House, Douglas.
The first modern office building in Douglas, built in 1972 on the site of the
Victory Hotel by Judah Binstock and later extended.

Securities; the next year he set up three of the newly-invented unit trusts, Pan Australian External, Pan Australian Minerals and Manx International Income. The unit trusts were subsequently passed to the Barclays Unicorn brand.

These, then, though initially designed for Island residents, were the first specifically offshore activities in the Isle of Man. There were no laws or regulations to monitor or control such activities until the introduction of the Prevention of Fraud (Investments) Act of 1968, which affected fund managers and others, and the Banking Act of 1975, which introduced not only control and licensing of banks, but, *inter alia*, the requirement for a Financial Advertising Licence, to be held by those who formed and sold Isle of Man companies. Neither was there any restriction

Judah Binstock.

on working or taking up employment in the Island until the Control of Employment Act of 1975.

Tax Planning, Tax Avoidance and Tax Evasion

But the opportunities offered by the Island's independent jurisdiction had not gone unnoticed. Even before the war, Isle of Man companies were regularly in use to hold the estates held by large landowners in Britain in order to convert the estates into foreign property and thereby exclude them from liability to Estate Duty, until the advantage was stopped in the Finance Act 1937. Manx companies were also used to receive the income of persons resident or domiciled outside the UK, such as by P.G. Wodehouse, by this time resident in France. Marlene Dietrich also usd a Manx company for her income, notably when she was making a film with Cary Grant directed by Alexander Korda (who is also believed to have used the Isle of Man), to be called *Knight Without Armour*. To Korda's fury

Dursley Stott and Douglas Bolton.

the film was never completed, owing to inattention on the part of the two principals who were clearly of the opinion that the film they were involved in should have been called *Night With Amour.* And again after the war Rothschild's, for instance, after looking around the world for a white Commonwealth country which was stable, English-speaking and within the European time zone, had been quietly making use of the Island for selected clients. They identified the Isle of Man Bank branch in Ramsey which in the 1960s had an able young manager, and used it for trust funds including those of a displaced European royal family. The Island had also been of use to foreigners who, like Marlene Dietrich, had acquired a residence here. Also fees at King William's College could be paid by UK residents out of foreign income without having a liability to UK income tax, since it was spent outside the UK. The absence of stamp duty and the exemption of foreign property from estate duty were additional incentives.

The Island's possibilities had also been identified by lawyers in England working in conjunction with Manx advocates and accountants. Patrick Taylor, a UK solicitor working with John Crellin at T. W. Cains, and later with Charles Cain, devised a number of highly complicated and technical tax schemes using Isle of Man companies and trusts, of a kind that would now be categorized as aggressive tax planning. Such schemes exploited weaknesses in UK revenue law enabling people to achieve tax savings quite legally, thereby foiling the intentions of successive chancellors, who, if the courts uphold the schemes, must then resort to devising anti-avoidance legislation, thus adding to the volume and complexity of the various UK tax and finance acts.

However, not all such tax-avoidance schemes were successful, as was shown by the internationally famous case of Furness and Dawson. This scheme, devised by John Crellin, involved a series of predetermined legally valid steps aimed at achieving the opposite result for tax purposes to that which would be achieved without taking the intermediate steps. The case was brought by the UK Inland Revenue seeking to have this artificial scheme set aside; it went to the Privy Council, who decided that, in such cases, the predetermined series of intermediate steps should be disregarded. Consequently, the scheme failed. The case established the leading precedent for discounting wholly artificial schemes. In Ireland, however, a similar scheme was devised for the artificial creation of capital gains tax losses by the successive use of a series of companies. This was known as the 'McGragh' scheme, and was successfully implemented using Isle of Man companies. The Irish Supreme Court chose to reject the legal precedent of the 'Imperial' House of Lords.

Although aggressive, this type of tax-planning scheme constituted a perfectly legitimate use of the Isle of Man's status. Many of those interested in tax schemes joined the International Tax Planning Association, where they could meet like-minded lawyers and accountants interested in using the Isle of Man or similar jurisdictions. However, there was no control of company formation until the provisions for Financial Advertising Licences in 1975, and companies were formed in profusion for possible future use. The names of many of these companies contained the word 'bank'; John Crellin recalls that Cains formed a number of companies with names such as Northern, Southern, Eastern, Western, and Central Bank, Savings and Investment Bank, and Peel City Bank, some of which were later used as actual banks. No permission was needed either to form or to operate a bank. It was not until 1975 that the first Banking Act was introduced providing for the licensing of banks. The long lists of company names of registered offices in the receptions of professional premises, often with exotic or absurd names, bore witness to the activity of company formation.

However, not all the schemes using companies and trusts operated from the Island were well planned. Many simply depended on concealment from the UK, Irish or other revenue authorities. This was easily achieved by using Manx professional or other directors and nominee shareholders, recorded at the General Registry (in the case of Manx companies), together with the registered office and company secretary. Accounts of private companies in the Island do not require filing other than with the Assessor of Income Tax; in the case of non-resident companies, owned by people outside the Island, with a business or investments outside the Island, and where the 'central management and control', as evidenced by board meetings, was outside the Island, the Assessor by concession did not require accounts, and from 1974, when the Company Registration Tax provisions were introduced, required only a fee and a simple return annually. Many professional directors of such companies regarded themselves as nominees carrying out the owners' instructions, and few formalities required under the Companies Acts, including accounts, were completed. It is not obligatory for the names of the real or beneficial owners to appear on any public record, or for them to be registered with the authorities.

Many non-resident companies failed to pay their non-resident Company Registration Tax, a sum of £200 per annum, and the long lists of defaulting companies published in the media by the Assessor of Income Tax, who was responsible for its collection, did little for the reputation of the Isle of Man. The most extreme examples of this practice were those companies registered in Sark with Sark 'nominee'

Government Offices, Douglas.
Built adjacent to Tynwald and the General Registry in the 1970s.
It displays most of the worst features of utilitarian offices.

directors, known as 'the Sark Lark'. Some directors had hundreds, if not thousands of companies, and signed whatever they were told to sign for a fee. Some 'registered offices' were located in huts at the bottom of people's gardens.

Unless there was some semblance of structure of ownership present in the form of trusts holding share capital, such companies were in effect simply perpetrating a fraud on the revenue of the country of the real, rather than the nominal, owners. The compliant directors were, in effect, a party to revenue fraud; indeed, if they were merely following orders, it might be argued that those who issued the instructions were the real directors, a concept which was later defined with the term 'shadow director'. Eventually UK company law made such shadow directors as responsible as the nominal directors for the acts of their companies. Even in the case of trusts, a trustee must take care to act in accordance with his trust rather than simply following orders. In addition, the paperwork frequently featured grave deficiencies in respect of board minutes, accounts, deeds of appointment, etc.[36] The rationale of structures was often absent from the files; even the document by means of which the company or trust was established was in many cases incomplete.

The concept of trusts originated in the English Law of Equity which dates back to the time of the crusades. Under this law, an individual (the settlor) entrusts assets, often as a protection, to another, (the trustee) 'in trust', to be held for the benefit often of widows or minor children (the beneficiaries). Nowadays, the legal owner is the trustee, although the beneficiaries are likely to be different. The settlor is no longer the actual owner. Generally, details of the settlor, the trustee and the classes of beneficiary are set out in the 'trust deed', i.e., the document recording the trust, even where the precise manner of applying the income or capital within the class of beneficiaries is left up to the discretion of the trustee. Manx trust law, both in theory and in practice, is similar to that of England, and this makes the use of Manx trusts simple and familiar for English users. In a correctly established trust, the change of ownership is genuine; and trusts are frequently used in tax-planning to own the share capital of underlying companies and property. But trust deeds are not public documents. In the 1970s and 1980s the parties were often unnecessarily concealed; trust deeds frequently had no named settlors, or else a corporate settlor, and no list of intended beneficiaries or classes of beneficiary, merely nominating a charity which it was not actually intended to benefit. These practices tend to show that whatever the genuine purposes of structures consisting of companies and trusts, unnecessary steps were taken to conceal the true owners, the true beneficiaries and the true purposes for which they were set up. This was typical of the approach by many of the professionals operating in the Isle of Man and elsewhere during the 1970s and 1980s.

'The Wild West without a Sheriff'

This may explain why the period between 1970 and 1982 in the Isle of Man has been described as the 'Wild West without a sheriff'. Some practitioners offered what was effectively blatant evasion, advertising internationally, preferably in In-Flight magazines. One particularly unscrupulous practitioner tried to pass himself off as a chartered accountant. Another colourful and notorious character, Chris Kingston,

Fort Anne, Douglas.
Designed by Ellis Brown around 1990 on the site of the much-loved
Fort Anne Hotel, it successfully echoes the old building above the harbour.

courted an outrageous reputation. He pioneered the practice of using groups of three companies, each owning the capital of the next, so that in effect there was no owner, until the authorities clamped down on such practices. He kept llamas and a pot-bellied Vietnamese pig. Kingston's tall, bearded figure cut a dash in a fedora and a long coat, and he was famous for the wild Christmas parties held at his Athol Street offices, with entertainment provided by strippers from Manchester. He once interviewed a potential employee dressed only in stockings, suspenders and a traffic cone to see whether she could cope with him (she couldn't); on another occasion, for some reason, he stabbed himself in his advocate's offices. Kingston eventually met his end by falling down a staircase in Portugal.

Kingston and his ilk, including drug dealers operating from addresses in the Island, attracted the attention of the national press and television. However, perhaps predictably, the media had little success in tracing the individuals or locating their offices.

However, the soubriquet of 'wild west' also reflects a very positive side and this has been the foundation of much of the Island's subsequent success. There were no real precedents and few guide lines: everyone had much to learn, practitioners and authorities alike. Mistakes were made, some bad. But without something of the 'wild west' spirit then it is unlikely that the Island would be so successful now.

New Initiatives in Finance

On 6th October 1969 Bill Dawson had taken up the newly-created post of Treasurer of the Isle of Man. His background and qualifications were that of Municipal Treasurer, a field of operation that was in many ways not unlike the Isle of Man with its system of Boards of Tynwald. However, the task that lay ahead of him was entirely different, as was impressed upon him from the outset. Sir Peter Stallard, who as Lieutenant-Governor was at the time still effectively the Island's Chief Executive and Chancellor of the Exchequer, advised him that his brief was to 'keep the Island from bankruptcy' and to prepare the Finance Board to take over responsibility for the Island's finances. J. B. Bolton, Chairman of the Finance Board (1967-76), also warned him that he must 'make sure the Island does not go bankrupt'.

His brief included the development of financial and other services which would effectively compensate for the continuing decline in tourism and also potentially act as insurance against the possible withdrawal of the largest contribution to the Island's tax revenues, which had long been provided by the Ronaldsway Aircraft Company. He was warned that his ideas would struggle to achieve the support of Tynwald because many members still refused to accept the decline of the lucrative visiting industry. Therein lay the rub: for although the new Treasurer had many good ideas, a number of which he was subsequently able to implement, he, like everyone else in the Island lacked the requisite experience, and Tynwald, as predicted, proved reluctant to support his innovations by ensuring the necessary provisions in respect of legislation, regulation and staffing.

The Island, both on the official and the corporate level, was feeling its way and inevitably mistakes were made. This exploratory phase of the development of the Island's financial services culminated in the collapse of the Savings and Investment Bank in June 1982 with debts of £42m. Many depositors lost heavily, and questions were raised within the international financial community about the safety and regulation of 'offshore' banking. This event highlighted the need for more rigorous financial supervision, and led to the establishment in 1983 of the Financial Supervision Commission within a proper legislative framework. The Manx Government was determined, in the aftermath of the SIB debacle, to project a favourable image so as to attract the right sort of business. In many ways it is remarkable how well the Island developed in the decade of the 70s despite the setback suffered by its reputation. Bill Dawson's ideas included a further reduction in income tax rates, the establishment of non-resident companies, the development of banking and insurance activities, a Freeport and a shipping register. All of these projects, along with many others, were to come to fruition in the course of time.

Besides the investment trusts and corporate activity, the first signs of the new developments were the establishment of the first two merchant banks, which opened in 1971 and 1972 respectively; these were Singer and Friedlander (Isle of Man), with David Lever as manager, and Slater Walker (Isle of Man) under returned Manxman Charles Cain. Although the parent company's problems caused Slater Walker to be sold in 1976, Charles Cain went on to found Charles Cain and Co. as a provider of trust and corporate services. Cain was also a pioneer of interesting corporate structures such as the Hybrid Company. He was elected to the House of Keys, he advocated the abolition of the Usury Acts, the proper control and licensing of banks, (achieved with the Banking Acts of 1975 and 1977), and the regulation of operators of trusts and companies in the Island, foreshadowing the Corporate Service Providers Act 2000 which would later empower the Financial Supervision Commission to regulate providers of services to companies registered in the Isle of Man.

Peveril Buildings, Douglas.
Built on the vacant site of the Peveril Hotel, opposite the Sea Terminal,
it is now the headquarters of Lloyd's Bank International.

Charles Cain also devised a way round the Usury Acts, which had existed in the Isle of Man since 1649 for fixing maximum rates of interest on borrowing by Act of Tynwald, which had long been stumbling-block for would-be investors. His tactic was the use of bills of exchange discounted at the appropriate rate, thus producing through the discount a similar rate of return to interest. This probably fell foul of the broad definition contained in Section 2 of the 1691 Usury Act, making him liable to the penalties prescribed under the Act's Section 3, i.e.: 'to forfeit and loose for every such Offence to the Lord of this Isle, and his Heires, the treble Value of the Moneys, Wares, Merchandizes, and other Things so lent, bargained, sold or exchanged' [*sic*]. By the time of the Usury Act 1968, the terminology had been modified, and interest rates capped at 8%. But 1970s inflation made the rate far too low, and in 1970 it was raised to 10%, and in 1974 to 12½%. By the legal restriction on rates of interest to below those available anywhere in the UK or elsewhere, the development of the banking sector was severely curtailed. Although unrealistic in the contemporary economic climate, the limits on interest were fiercely protected by Members of Tynwald, despite determined efforts on the part of the Treasurer and bankers for repeal. The Acts were not finally repealed until 10th July 1979.

Exchange Control

Exchange Control was also a very important factor in the growth of the Island's economy. The UK Exchange Control Act 1947 had introduced exchange control, restricting the movement of currency or capital, for the whole of the sterling area, which comprised the British Isles and English-speaking Empire and Commonwealth. But in June 1972, partly as a consequence of decimalization, the scheduled territories of the sterling area were reduced to the British Isles including Ireland, the Channel Islands and the Isle of Man, with Gibraltar added the following year. In consequence, it became very difficult to move larger sums of money beyond the British Isles; the banks of Jersey, Guernsey and Man were available for those who wished to keep their funds outside the United Kingdom. This was one of the principal reasons for the sudden increase in the number of banks in the Isle of Man; the other reason was an extra-statutory concession, made by the Assessor on 18th May 1973, exempting bank interest paid by banks to non-residents from liability to Manx tax.

As a footnote to the question of exchange control, the purchase of dollars was subject to payment of a dollar premium, only part of which was recoverable in the event of subsequent resale. An associate of Judah Binstock fell foul of British law when he devised a method of counteracting this apparent inequity; this was the point at which Judah Binstock took the prudent precaution of removing himself to southern Spain; he was to play little further part in the development of the Isle of Man, and was clearly nervous of the possible consequences of the dollar premium refund scheme; for he was recognised by Dr Gordon Moore, brother of the retired Deemster, in a restaurant in France, just over the border with Spain, and, to avoid any risk of being found in a country where an extradition treaty with the UK existed, returned to Spain immediately without finishing his meal.

Banking

The new measures just described also saw the formation of a series of new banks. Some of the clearing banks formed new, deposit-taking subsidiaries, such as Barclays Finance Company (Isle of Man) and Midland Bank Trust Corporation (Isle of Man). Williams and Glyn's Bank (IOM), established in 1973, was to become part of Royal Bank of Scotland in 1984; from the start this bank demonstrated a heightened awareness of the opportunities offered by banking.[37] Besides subsidiaries of UK and other banking groups, mention should be made of the first transatlantic bank, The Royal Trust of Canada, later taken over by the Royal Bank of Canada. In particular, the 1970s marked the establishment of a series of locally-owned private banks only one of which survived the 1980s.

The Banking Acts of 1975 and 1977 regulated the licensing of banks and the conducting of banking business. Amongst other things, they provided for the restriction of the use of the word 'bank' and the conducting of a banking business within or from the Isle of Man. The Finance Board and the Treasurer of the Isle of Man were given the responsibility for ensuring that those who conducted such business were fit and proper persons, with adequate capital, that they employed fit and proper managers had adequate reporting systems, and that their business was viable. Regulations were established and licences issued, yet no requirement was made for supervision, let alone provision for the suspension of licences. Even though statistical returns were made, which, had the Treasurer or his Commercial Relations Officer possessed the time or knowledge to study them, could have alerted them to any problems that arose, the banks were virtually self-regulating. The Treasurer could not be held solely accountable for the failure of the system, although, because of his inexperience he laid both himself and the Island open to the disasters which befell within seven years of the introduction of the 1975 Banking Act. The Treasurer and the Finance Board struggled to get legislation passed by a largely reluctant Tynwald, who baulked at approving the expense of establishing an appropriate supervisory framework of legislation and supervision, until they were compelled to do so by sheer necessity.

Insurance

The third area of development within the financial services sector during this period was in offshore insurance. The Companies Act 1974 introduced provisions for the authorization and supervision by the Finance Board of Manx companies carrying on insurance business. The Income Tax Act 1978 exempted such companies from income tax on their underwriting profits, although investment income remained liable. This competitive disadvantage of taxation of investment income was removed by the passing of the Exempt Insurance Companies Act 1981. The insurance companies that were being attracted were largely so-called 'captive' insurance companies, that is, insurance companies that generally insure only part of the risk of a group of companies, or an association of firms or persons that are also their owners, or which write risks whose origins are restricted or to which it has unique access. They can take on the insurance of part of a group's risk that cannot be obtained in the insurance market, or can be obtained more economically, and are thus able to build up tax-free profits and resources for the group or association, and to help to control the incidence of losses or accidents within a group. Before 1981, a few Manx captives were formed, but after the 1981 Act their numbers increased considerably. The privatisation of utilities in the UK contributed to this development, attracting to the Island well-known companies such as British Gas and Yorkshire Water.

A second category of offshore insurance companies also came to the Isle of Man. These were long-term endowment life insurance companies, which initially were kept out of the scope of Manx tax for non-resident policy holders in order to encourage the sector. The such first company to be established was Lloyds Life, established by the Lloyds market in Castletown in 1981; this later became Royal Life, and, later still, Friends Provident Life. The development of this very important sector of the financial services industry will be dealt with later. Suffice it to say here that the insurance industry has not been plagued with the disasters which at various times befell sections of the banking industry.

It is, however, worth mentioning two Isle of Man Assurance operations which did cause a certain amount of controversy. The first was the St Christopher's policy, under which drivers who had lost their driving licence for road traffic offences could have a chauffeur provided under their insurance policy. In the end, this was considered against public policy, and was stopped.

The second example was the Holiday Property Bond; this provided policy holders (of a small life assurance element) with free holiday accommodation. In practice, along with a number of other savings schemes effective through nominal life assurance policies, the scheme was a sort of unit trust, the dividends of which were enjoyed in the form of holidays. However, it attracted unwelcome attention in the media; the *Daily Mirror* threw the scheme open to question and the BBC produced a critical rapportage; the scheme was subjected to scrutiny by the authority of the Insurance Supervisor. But, apart from very high initial charges[38] which are not obvious to the user from a cursory perusal of the promotional literature, and apart from the fact that future income from the investment element would not meet the costs, once certain adjustments had been made to the scheme, the criticism proved to be largely unfounded. The scheme continues to flourish. In many ways it was superior to the timeshare concept for which the Island provided trustees and operators. In the early days, these activities, too, had been controversial. The reported cases of malpractice in that industry were not confined to the Isle of Man, but some Island-based practitioners on the Island were the object of criticism. The conducting of timeshare business was finally brought under control under the Timeshare Act of 1996.

Customs and Excise

Throughout the period from 1960 to 1980, and even later, the question of the Common Purse Agreement formed the subject of much heated debate, the strongest representations being made in favour of an end to the Agreement by cancellation, or abrogation. The arguments advanced in favour of abrogation were principally these: firstly, it was maintained that while the Island's principal sources of revenue, which by this time were VAT and excise, were regulated from Westminster with no regard for the Island's particular needs, the Island could not claim to have independent political control of its affairs; secondly, it was postulated that VAT and duty affected the viability of the tourist industry, especially by comparison with the Channel Islands where it was not levied; and the faster vessels now available raise the possibility of 'booze cruises' as found on the Channel.

Those who opposed the abolition of the Common Purse Agreement were people involved in the manufacturing sector and also the finance industry. Tynwald commissioned PA International Management Consultants to examine the agreement and recommend a course of action. Their report, published in 1976, made the recommendation that the Agreement should be terminated. This provoked an outcry from manufacturers, who protested that, if customs formalities were to be imposed between the Island and the UK, necessitating full customs formalities and documentation for all movements of goods on or off the Island, and the bureaucratic costs and delays involved, the resultant cost to manufacturers would force them to move their operations out of the Island. In the event, the only one of the consultants' recommendations to be adopted was that the Isle of Man and its own officers should assume responsibility for Customs and Excise, and the Customs and Excise should be locally administered, even if in accordance with UK rules.

The Island did not become part of the European Union when Britain and Ireland acceded in 1972. Instead, it entered into a special relationship of semi-detachment under Protocol 3 of the Treaty of Rome, as did the Channel Islands. In practice, many European Union directives are adopted by the Island, in many cases to facilitate exports, for example of agricultural products, which must comply with European requirements. There is, however, a view that Tynwald is too ready to adopt wholesale all laws and regulations emanating not only from the European Union but also from the United Kingdom. Occasionally, small variations in respect of non-exportable services are negotiated with the UK with the permission of the European Union.

It is interesting to note that, under the Customs and Excise Agreement (as the Common Purse Agreement was renamed in 1979), the strong revenues from indirect taxation have enabled the Island to counter the attacks on discriminatory taxes for companies in the form of tax exemption for 'offshore' companies. Even as late as 1994 when the Central Economic Strategy Unit, a 'think tank' was set up at the suggestion of Terry Groves MHK, Minister of Local Government and the Environment, comprising prominent members from all areas of economic activity in the Island, there was almost no support for abrogation.

Despite these various initiatives, by the end of the 1970s the economy was flat and the property market stagnant. The Treasurer was under pressure from the new Finance Board to attract new financial activities and institutions; little did anyone expect the impending cataclysm encapsulated in the collapse of the Savings and Investment Bank.

CHAPTER 6

COLLAPSE AND CRISIS

Banking Disasters

In the early 1980s in the Island there occurred a number of banking disasters. In a minute dated 6th April 1973 on the Development of the Island's Finance Sector, the Treasurer, Bill Dawson, wrote:

> In recent months several merchant banks have been established here and their very presence, with their wide and usually progressive approach to banking and finance, will do much in establishing the Island as a financial centre. This injection of new management is advantageous, and may lead to the development of international financial business, which is sadly missing at the moment. In my recent talks with bank managers of the clearing banks, there was abundant evidence of the lack of any dynamic approach by the banking fraternity to develop the international side of the bank. ...
>
> The United Kingdom clearing banks appear to be content to channel surplus funds of their Isle of Man branches through to their subsidiaries in Jersey. While such a policy may be convenient for the clearing banks, it is not in the interest of the Manx economy.

These words encapsulate the Island's dilemma. Leading British banks displayed little interest in encouraging their Manx operations to take advantage of the Island's distinctive status. Indeed, Lombard Bank, part of the Nat-West group, was not allowed to advertise outside the Isle of Man. This stance was to persist well into the 1980s. The attitude displayed by Sir Timothy Bevan, Chairman of Barclays, was typically unimaginative: he stated that Barclays used the Channel Islands for all their offshore work.[39] Apart from one Irish bank and one Canadian bank, The Royal Trust, and the handful of merchant banks, many of which concentrated on investment management, no foreign banks were represented on the Island until the Bank of Credit and Commerce International SA opened a branch in 1979.

Savings and Investment Bank, Upper Church Street, Douglas in 1982.

It was against this background that a number of private banks were established in the Island and began trading; this was to have momentous consequences. Many of these banks ran into difficulties, others closed, while others again were subsumed into larger groups and thus continue in effect to exist to the present day. Only one privately-owned bank, Celtic Bank, established by Albert Gubay in 1977, survives in its original form.

When some private banks ran into difficulties it caused the Island's authorities some measure of concern, but these banks' problems had comparatively little impact on the Island, largely because their losses were relatively small. The International Financial Trust Corporation Limited, founded in the early 1970s by a firm of chartered accountants, Midgeley Snelling, failed in September 1981 because of injudicious loans that proved difficult to recover. In the event, depositors recovered 98% of their deposits. After the collapse of the Savings and Investment Bank in June 1982, several more banks closed; these included Investors Mercantile Finance Limited (or IMF), Chancellor Finance (Isle of Man) Limited, Kingsnorth Bank, which had acquired Fitzwilliam Bank in 1980, and Irish

Overseas Bank Limited. The short-lived Falcon Bank Isle of Man Limited had, incredibly, been granted a banking licence in 1979, actually before its incorporation with an issued share capital of £2.

Savings and Investment Bank

The Savings and Investment Bank Limited (SIB) had been incorporated on 18th December 1965 by T. W. Cains, advocates, as one of a batch of shelf companies whose names included the word 'bank', with an issued share capital of £2 out of an authorised share capital of £2,000. It was almost a decade later that the SIB was acquired and began operating as a public company with an increased share capital of £210,000 issued on 29th August 1975. Later the same year it obtained a banking licence under Section 3 of the new Banking Act. The shares were held fairly widely in the Island, but the concept and control lay in the hands of the Harper family, partners of Sugdens, a leading firm of chartered accountants.[40] The bank's facilities were extensively used by other professionals, both by fellow partners of Sugdens and their successor firms, and by advocates, especially for banking monies related to schemes devised for the avoidance or evasion of taxes, chiefly British and Irish taxes. In those days, before money-laundering and assisting in tax evasion schemes were considered criminal, the Island's facilities were widely exploited for such purposes, either directly or through offshore private companies. These activities frequently featured 'back-to-back' schemes, whereby a deposit with a bank by one person or company was matched by an equivalent loan to another person or company. Such schemes are not in themselves illegal, and may constitute a legitimate tool in tax-planning, but they were to prove an added complication in the event of liquidations.

At this point a review of the prevailing economic climate might prove helpful. During the period of the Heath Government of 1970-1974, spilling over into the ensuing period of Labour government, the 'dash for growth' designed to accelerate the UK economy through the preceding cycles of 'boom and bust' had proved unsuccessful, resulting in the first experience of high inflation; a collapse of the property and share market

*Bill Dawson, Treasurer of the Isle of Man
from 1969.*

followed in its wake. One consequence of this had been the secondary
banking collapse, which severely affected the City of London. The British
Government was compelled to rescue a number of smaller banks so as to
prevent their collapse from triggering a general banking collapse with
disastrous effects on the British economy and the City of London. The
crisis showed that the City's traditional gentlemanly ways of conducting
business were no longer adequate, and in 1975 the Bank of England
instituted a system of inspection. The Isle of Man did not follow the
UK's example until 1983, when it experienced its own banking crisis, and
established the Financial Supervision Commission, with professional
banking supervision by suitably experienced people.

Before 1983 banks in the Isle of Man continued to be virtually self-
regulating. Statistical returns were sent to the Treasury, but these were
often late and were not closely examined, despite a growing awareness
within the Treasury that the SIB, in particular, was experiencing
difficulties from time to time. But, even where supervisors are aware that

a bank is in difficulties, as the problems multiply, finding a solution to them becomes progressively more difficult to achieve. The authorities' dilemma is not dissimilar to that of a bank faced by a bad debt; if the debt is small, the bank can call it in, or refuse to advance further sums to the debtor; but if the debt increases to a point where it threatens to destabilize the bank, further loans are often made to avoid precipitating the very event caused by the debt itself. It is the same with supervising authorities: in the UK's secondary banking crisis of 1975, collapses were averted by the provision of support and credit sufficient to allow banks to ride out the collapses of asset values. But the Isle of Man Government possessed neither the resources nor the competence to envisage this level of support, nor were they able to persuade other banks to come to their assistance. They were finally advised that the SIB was in such a parlous state that it was beyond saving.

The SIB had been in trouble before its ultimate collapse. The original directors had cherished the ambition of competing with the Isle of Man Bank in the provision of loans to Isle of Man businesses. One of these projects was a loan of around one million pounds in connexion with the rebuilding of the Fort Anne Hotel under the management of Roger Brown. However, the site proved unstable and the project was mismanaged, leaving the bank with a debt of one million pounds and a worthless security. With the knowledge of the government Treasurer, Bill Dawson, in March 1977 Tom Whipp, who had moved to the Island with his family, (one of whom, Peter Whipp, had qualified as a chartered accountant with Sugdens), declared himself willing to acquire the shares of the SIB for 25p, his own estimate of their value. He received help from the Treasurer in the form of a tax concession, contrary to the technical opinion of the Assessor of Income Tax, Mark Solly, and the Attorney General, Jack Corrin, with the effect that the additional funding required to refinance the SIB to the tune of £950,000 could be set as an expense against the income from other family interests; in effect, Tom Whipp received a government subsidy amounting to some £200,000. The Harper family made good the losses of outside shareholders at a cost of £472,000. The depositors were, for the moment, protected.

The economy of the Isle of Man became less buoyant at the end of the 1970s, and this flatness continued until the mid 1980s. Fewer wealthy new residents were coming to the Island. The election of Margaret Thatcher's Conservative Government in 1979, with the prospect of tax cuts and the removal of exchange control, eliminated some of the chief incentives for people to leave the UK. Furthermore, it was now twenty years since the arrival in the Island of the first wave of new residents. In the interim, many had died, and their survivors were returning to the UK, releasing a surplus of housing stock, much of which was poorly built and in bad repair; property prices slumped. Neither could the Island's financial sector be said to be flourishing. The situation created a sense that urgent measures were called for to support and promote financial services. Unsurprisingly, the solution to the first SIB crisis was accepted with relief by both the Finance Board and the Treasurer.

It is easy to criticise the handling of this first crisis; the directors were not experienced bankers, nor did they have at their disposal either the capital or the resources for lending on a large scale. The Treasurer successfully found a solution to the crisis in 1979. He should have been alert to the possibility of a recurrence, and perhaps this failure to monitor and learn from the fate of the SIB in particular constitutes the most telling indictment. But the Treasurer was not a supervisor; he did not have the staff, and his principal brief, after all, was to manage the Island's finances. It should be remembered that, even with all the resources of the Bank of England at its disposal, Britain had experienced the collapses of secondary banks and deposit takers in the 1970s, and was to be caught out again by the collapses of two major institutions, Barings in 1995 and the Bank of Credit and Commerce International SA, in July 1991 and has experienced similar problems with Northern Rock in 2007 without demonstrating the ability to avoid or solve the crises.

SIB Changes Hands - Again

The Whipp family's ownership of the SIB was of short duration. In December 1977, the same year in which they had acquired it, they agreed to sell it to a specially-formed trust, the Mayflower Trust. To facilitate the purchase, the bank lent the Mayflower Trust the purchase price of £1,717,700. It will be immediately apparent that a loan to pay for a company's share capital borrowed from that same company prima facie contravenes Section 45 of the Companies Act 1931, which states:

> it shall not be lawful for a company to give, whether directly or indirectly, and whether by means of loan, guarantee, the provision of security, or otherwise, any financial assistance for the purpose of or in connection with a purchase made, or to be made, by any person of any shares in the company

However, Subsection (a) of the Act contains the proviso 'that nothing in this section shall be taken to prohibit, where the lending of money is part of the ordinary business of a company, the lending of money by the company in the ordinary course of its business'. In the case of the SIB, both parties, vendors and purchasers, claimed that they relied on this proviso. The loan was duly made to Mayflower, providing some measure of notional security through connected interests, and the cash remained on deposit with the bank until its withdrawal by Tom Whipp in January 1982. What had in fact happened, of course, was that the effective capital of the bank had been reduced by £1.7 million, converted into what proved to be a very insecure loan to the Mayflower Trust which owned the share capital. Notwithstanding, the Treasurer sanctioned the transfer of the banking licence to the bank's new owners.

Who were the parties behind this new structure and ownership? The Mayflower Trust was a fairly conventional discretionary trust in favour of beneficiaries who were not fully defined in the trust deed. The legal work was prepared by a Nottingham solicitor, Norman Ashton-Hill, and by Colin Fick and Mark Moroney, Manx advocates, of Callow and Fick. Norman Ashton-Hill was a legal adviser to Victor Gray, whose holdings included Graylaw, an extensive garage business with some 200 sites in the South of England which had occasionally experienced liquidity problems. Gray and another adviser, Robert Killen, a banker, became aware of the SIB's potential as a source of cheap bridging finance for Gray's business interests, and as a vehicle for the transfer of his interests offshore. Despite the convoluted web of Gray's organization, as far as the SIB was concerned, the ownership of the bank by Mayflower Trust, acquired with money lent to Mayflower by the bank, remained the essence of the structure.

In this way the SIB came into the effective ownership of Victor Gray. Acting Deemster Field Fisher, in his judgement of 25th April 1990, made it clear that the government knew this from the beginning of Gray's involvement; and although Gray strenuously denied this, it was to Gray to whom the Treasurer, accompanied by three partners from Pannell Kerr Forster, went in July 1982 at an address in Finsbury Square, London, in an effort to negotiate a rescue operation in conjunction with the Thai Farmers Bank and other banks. The new bank board contained many of Gray's advisers. The chairman of the board was Archie Lyle, who had also been chairman of Albert Gubay's Celtic Bank and IMF, and had had a career in banking. The managing director was Robert Killen, who effectively ran the bank's affairs. The other executive who had an important input into the day-to-day running of the bank was John Cunningham. Stuart Callister, Mr Whelan and the legal advisers Norman Ashton-Hill and Mark Moroney were non-executive directors; in practice, the non-executive directors appeared to have little say in the conducting of the bank's business. Grey was not a member of the board, though he very occasionally appeared at board meetings. It would appear that Robert Killen acquired to an increasing degree the habit of taking decisions on loans with little if any consultation with the board. The Board Minutes can only be described as cursory; they contained little evidence of loans made, or difficulties encountered with the security of such loans. It would have been reasonable to have expected board members who were professional bankers and lawyers to demand proper information and a full review of the bank's affairs, including a detailed review of all loans, or to resign. In practice, some measure of concern was expressed, and, shortly before the collapse, Mark Moroney did request a report from the auditors, the local firm of Clarke & Rayton.

The partner in charge of this assignment, Michael Crowe, was ill-equipped to carry out the task successfully. A relatively young man, he had little experience of dealing with the kind of people who were in charge of the bank, like Gray and Killen, and was unfamiliar with the highly specialized business of bank audits.[41] Even when the auditors raised valid points, for example, when they expressed dissatisfaction with the transactions (achieved by transfers of over-valued assets) involved in re-capitalizing the bank, and consequently threatened on 2nd April 1981 to express their doubts in a qualification in the audit report on the 1980 accounts, in May they allowed themselves to be persuaded into signing an unqualified audit report. Indeed, the inspectors[42] (Chadwick et al) appointed to investigate the SIB's affairs after its collapse believed the bank had been insolvent even in 1979, after disallowing the £1.7m loan to Mayflower as irrecoverable through illegality, and an adjustment to take into account the 'window-dressing' amounting to £2.2m of loans to Gray's companies, temporarily repaid over the year end. After these adjustments, the inspectors calculated there was a net deficit of £100,000 at the end of 1979. By the end of 1980, they calculated a deficit of £2.7m, and, at the end of 1981, they calculated that the provision for bad loans should have been somewhere in the region of £10m. By the time of the report presented by the Government auditors in July 1982, the provision required was estimated at around £20m, or approximately half the loan book of around £42m.

Even though the Board, the Government and the public were lulled into a sense of security by the auditors' clean audit reports, the returns made to the Commercial Relations Officer, viewed in the light of the bank's chequered history and the manner of its change of ownership, should have alerted both him and the Treasurer to the need for action.

The transfer of the licence itself was the first cardinal error, at a time when the bank was temporarily stable in the hands of the Whipps. Though the Treasurer's office was written into the Banking Act 1975 as bearing responsibility for the issue of banking and other licences, and for the supervision of the proper conduct of banks generally, neither he nor his Commercial Relations Officer, Peter Duncan, a chartered accountant, had any experience of banking supervision; nor, when the figures on the inadequate statistical returns revealed obvious problems, did either the Treasurer or the Commercial Relations Officer take steps to control the situation. Instead, they continued to devote their energies to what they perceived, correctly, to be their principal duties: Bill Dawson, as Treasurer, managing the Island's finances, Peter Duncan, as Commercial Relations Officer, promoting the Island's financial services, particularly through attracting new business, a role in inherent conflict with supervision. The inspectors reported:

> The returns indicated that SIB was insolvent in February 1981 and also in August and November of that year... we would have expected some enquiry to have been made both at the bank and by the Treasury, in order to ascertain whether the return was accurate...we have found no evidence of any enquiry of this nature.[43]

Collapse of SIB

By 1982 the problems were getting worse. By June, when the bank closed, the auditors had been unable to complete their audit. Advances were now in the region of £42m, and even Robert Killen was attempting to call some of them in. Liberal amounts of money had been advanced, not only to Mayflower and Graylaw interests as previously, but also to a series of companies or groups that spent lavishly but appeared to possess few assets. Among these advances was a series of property loans amounting to £1m made through a man named Kelsey, an intermediary, ostensibly with a view to avoiding Development Land Tax through the use of offshore structures; this money was recycled and vanished. Michael Morris, together with an accomplice, Fincken, acquired Medway, a scrap metal subsidiary of British Anzani, assisted by loans of nearly £5m, now believed to have been largely for the principals' personal spending. British Anzani was a property and construction company that had suffered in the 1974 property slump. In June 1982 the group owed SIB over £7m. Work on the homes of Messrs Fincken and Morris represented virtually the sole construction contracts the group had obtained. Stephen Kendall Lane, whom Morris and Fincken were attempting to remove from International Car Hire, records: 'I was advised that I would receive no compensation, and Mr Fincken and Mr Morris, in Mr Killen's presence, informed me that, if I did sell my story, I would (a) have my face and throat slashed and (b) find £350,000 of personal drawings against my name.'[44]

Gil Hunter (whose various aliases included the names Edward Lee, Francis Ma, Michael Stall, John Dugay, John Douglas, Ted Denham and John Brown) was another major debtor; in June 1982 his group owed some £4.7m. Hunter had moved to the Island in the mid-1970s after being declared bankrupt in England; the most notorious of his various ventures was the lavish restoration of a Douglas promenade boarding house, the Regent Hotel, as the Admiral's Rest (now Admiral House) at a cost of £1m. Fearing a conviction for conspiracy to defraud the Inland Revenue, he fled the Island in December 1981 in dramatic style, abandoning his red Rolls Royce on the runway at Ronaldsway before flying to the South of Spain in a chartered Lear Jet.

Another £2m was lent to Eurofurn, a Maltese kitchen company, for the manufacture of doors for kitchen cabinets; the one door that was ever actually produced by the company was discovered in the SIB boardroom in June 1982.

Two factors triggered the SIB denouement; firstly, Philip Brown, who had previous involvement with the bank and some of Hunter's companies, presented to the Treasurer a dossier of allegations of forgery and serious irregularities. Killen and Cunningham, and later, on 22nd March 1982, the whole board, were interviewed. They strenuously denied Brown's accusations, casting aspersions on his veracity. The Treasurer was inclined to believe the board rather than Brown's allegations; T. W. Cain & Co was threatened with a libel suit. As Peter Crellin of Cain's stated to the inspectors:

> It was apparent they were trying to take it seriously, but they thought they had no powers, since no bank inspector had been appointed under the provisions of the Act; they were advertising for the appointment of a part-time inspector and considered until there was an inspector, there was not very much they could do.[45]

The inspectors disagreed with this view, stating: 'if the Treasurer intended to suggest to Crellin that he had no power to inspect the Bank's records, we think he was mistaken - see sections 5 (1), (2) and (5) of the Banking Act 1975'.

However the final straw was the attempt to recover a loan of £5m advanced to Gasco, a company connected to Jim Raper, established for the acquisition of the shares of St Piran, a listed mining company. SIB attempted to seize the St Piran shares which were the security for the loan. Jim Raper retaliated with a press release in June 1982 in which he alleged that SIB was insolvent, thus precipitating a run on the bank. On June 16th Barclays refused to honour SIB cheques; on June 22nd Barclays examined the SIB books and reported: 'Basically the situation appeared to be one of complete muddle, and it seemed to us there was no-one in SIB who really knew how to run a bank'.[46] On midday of Friday 25th June 1982 the Treasurer withdrew the bank's licence and it closed.

Awareness of the bank's difficulties had posed problems for officials of the established banks. The awareness was, as is often the case, based on probability, not certainty. There were, subsequently, reports that discreet attempts had been made to warn off people making or leaving deposits with the SIB. In one case, a client who was on his way to deposit £10m with a clearing bank, found that the doors had just closed; but, on driving on, he saw the SIB open and offering good interest on deposits and so deposited the whole amount with there. When the manager of the clearing bank asked him the next day why he hadn't brought in the expected £10m, and he learned that the client had placed the entire amount in the SIB, half for one month and the remainder for three months, the manager persuaded him to give the appropriate notice. £5m was rescued, but the SIB then crashed and the remaining £5m was lost. So easy it was to be caught out. It was clear that, many people refused to believe the evidence and were still making deposits at the eleventh hour, lured by the promise of higher interest rates, a fact which meant there was little sympathy from the Manx public generally after the crash. Another story claims that the Bishop of Sodor and Man, tipped off by an SIB bank employee, left Government House in the middle of an official luncheon in order to remove his personal deposit, and returned to the luncheon having done so.

Government Reaction

The first many members of Tynwald knew of the crisis was a

summons from the Lieutenant-Governor as President of Tynwald to a meeting of Tynwald in private session. Tony Brown, later Speaker of the House of Keys and subsequently Chief Minister, then a very young and newly-elected member for Castletown, recalls the police being sent out to find members for a meeting that afternoon. The initial shock caused by this unprecedented crisis was followed by concern for the Island's reputation. There was a real sense of urgency. At that time, before the Island adopted the ministerial system, Tynwald itself was the Government of the Isle of Man, all the chairmen and members of the various boards of Tynwald were also members of Tynwald.

The Manx Government, unsure what to believe about the extent of the bank's problems, decided to commission an enquiry by their own auditors, Pannell Kerr Forster (PKF), who both as themselves and as W. H. Walker & Co had been Government auditors since 1886. By far the largest firm of accountants on the Island, PKF audited over a dozen of the Island's banks. Twenty-five chartered accountants from their staff entered the bank on the day of closure, with the brief of examining its affairs with a critical eye, yet at the same time with a view to advising the Government as to the feasibility of saving the bank, and, in the event such a rescue were considered possible, to estimating its cost.[47] Within two weeks, despite difficulties in carrying out their work, the auditors had amassed sufficient evidence to allow the Government to make an informed decision. One of the things they noticed was the vast amount of shredding of records that appeared to be going on. Valerie Cottle, a local journalist, went to the bank's premises on Upper Church Street in hopes of being able to reconstruct evidence, carrying away sacks that had been left in the back lane, but without success. PKF, however, found a largely complete set of books which enabled them to form an accurate assessment of the situation, despite the absence from the bank safe of items listed in the books such as 'cash', 'travellers cheques' and 'bills of exchange'.[48]

All in all, the state of affairs was much as described above, with a prima facie deficit of some £20m, or half the bank's assets. In the event of actual liquidation, the picture would be even bleaker. The complicated structures of loans and matching security, and the validity of the charges and of the 'back-to-back' loans and deposits, presented particular difficulties. The accountants reported their findings to a full meeting of the Finance Board. The Government was seeking some way out of the crisis which would not entail undertaking to make good the entire deficit at tax-payers' expense. They hoped a consortium of banks would come to the rescue, but the situation had deteriorated to a point where this was clearly not going to happen, and on 2nd August 1982, SIB was put into liquidation. Ultimately, only £8m of the loans were ever recovered. By the year 2000, depositors had recovered 33p in the pound, together with 50% of deposits under £5,000, paid ex gratia by the Government at a cost of £4.5m. Some depositors, afraid of inviting repercussions if their names were made public, never claimed in the liquidation; in fact, only some 1,600 out of 3,000 depositors claimed; of a total of £42.2m deposited, £6.6m remained unclaimed.

The SIB closure caused an immediate uproar. Two depositors in particular led the protests, demanding that the Government should compensate depositors in full on the grounds that depositors had relied upon the implied supervision inherent in the granting and renewal of SIB's banking licence. Within the Island, however, there was a strong feeling that, whatever the deficiencies of the supervision, banking licences were not guarantees, and that any sensible person should realize that the higher rates of interest paid by small private banks must carry greater risk; it would be inequitable to compensate people who had used this bank to benefit from its higher interest rates for their error of judgement. The collapse made national headlines in the UK. Shortly afterwards in 1983 the speakers on a Manx Government road show which visited London, Bristol and Edinburgh to extol the merits of the Island's financial services, found themselves obliged to make a discreet entrance through a side door to dodge a demonstration by protesters, orchestrated by one depositor, Gwendoline Lamb, outside the main entrance.

The Manx Government at first refused to make good any part of the depositors' losses. However, a small payment was eventually made in 1992. In fact the Government was in no position to offer any assistance to depositors, even had it so wished, since it possessed no funds beyond the

Dr Edgar Mann, Chairman of the Finance Board, 1981-85,
Chairman of Executive Council, 1985-86.

one million pounds of reserves, and the bank deposits amounted to forty
million pounds, at least half of which was likely to be at risk. Dr Edgar
Mann[49] did attempt to place the Government in a position to be able to
offer limited assistance to depositors, by approaching Edward Brownsden,
the Chairman of the Isle of Man Bank, which had been the Government's
bankers for a century, requesting an advance of four million pounds at
concessionary rates. Dr Mann was not permitted to attend the meeting of
the bank's board, but was left sitting in a passage while they considered his
request. Amazingly, the request was refused out of hand, let alone at
concessionary rates, on the grounds that the Isle of Man Bank took no
responsibility for the Government's crisis and saw no reason why it should
help out with a loan of any kind, still less at concessionary rates. The fact
that the Isle of Man Bank, like other clearing banks, had steadfastly and

successfully opposed both any form of supervision under the Banking Act and the appointment of a supervisor carried no weight; nor did the presence on the bank's board of two members of the Finance Board who had presumably authorised the approach.[50]

But the Government had to act, and did so decisively. They immediately appointed two experienced Bank of England inspectors, Richard Farrant and Wendy Hyde, to investigate and report and, in October 1982, Dr Martin Owen to replace Peter Duncan, who had resigned as Commercial Relations Officer in May of that year. Jim Noakes and Duncan Neil were appointed as supervisors from 1 January 1983. The Farrant/Hyde Report was completed by December 1982, but not published until May 1990, after the collapse of the trial of the bank officers.

Inspectors were also appointed to report on the circumstances leading to the collapse of the bank; these were J. M. Chadwick, QC, a specialist on financial matters, Michael Jordan, of liquidation specialists Cork Gully, and John Beer of Peat Marwick, who were also the liquidators of the bank. It was hoped to keep costs down, but the compilation of the report probably took longer in consequence, taking three and a half years to complete. The report was jealously guarded; even the Attorney General and the police had difficulty in obtaining or retaining a copy, and this delayed criminal proceedings. Moreover, the report contained material on financial matters that was both extensive and complex, although not, in the writer's opinion, so complex as to be beyond the comprehension of either the police or the Attorney General both of whom later claimed they were not capable of understanding it.[51] In addition, the Government auditors' investigation had provided sufficient documentation to furnish prima facie evidence, and the auditors had offered their assistance to the inspectors, the Government and the police. In July 1983, they had, incidentally, in the absence of a fraud squad, assisted the police in preparing a criminal case against chartered accountant Richard Brooks, of Harding, Thompson, Brooks & Co., who had misrepresented to his clients that he had invested some £2m in containers, whereas in fact he had appropriated it for his personal use, acquiring property in the Isle of Man, through companies. His timing was disastrous and he was unable to repay his clients. He fled to Spain, but was pursued by Detective Inspector Platt and Detective Sergeant Kneale who found him camping in straightened circumstances in development property in Marbella; despite having no jurisdiction in Spain and the absence of any extradition treaty they managed to persuade him to return to the Island to stand trial. He pleaded guilty and was sent to prison.[52]

The SIB saga took a long time to resolve. Whereas, when Dumbell's Bank failed in 1900, its officers were tried and imprisoned within eight months of the bank's closure, the SIB trial did not start until March 1990, almost eight years after the SIB's collapse. An elderly retired QC, Thomas Field Fisher, presided as Acting Deemster over an unlikely *ad hoc* courtroom created in the Ocean Castle Hotel in Port Erin. The defendants were Michael Crowe, the auditor; Robert Killen and John Cunningham, executives of SIB; Norman Ashton-Hill and Mark Moroney, non-executive directors; Graylaw accountants Stanley Grafham and Dennis Finfer, and Victor Gray himself. The Chairman, Archie Lyle, had died some two years previously. It might well have been argued that several of those arraigned were guilty of naïvety, perhaps to the point of negligence, rather than malpractice, and that the trial should have focussed from the outset upon those principally and knowingly involved, namely Victor Gray, Robert Killen and John Cunningham. After about a month of preliminary pleadings, Victor Gray contracted a serious illness which his lawyers claimed prevented his standing trial, and proceedings against him were temporarily suspended pending his recovery. Finally, on 25th April 1990, the Acting Deemster, to general dismay, stayed the trial of all the defendants on the grounds that the delay in the proceedings had seriously prejudiced their chances of a fair trial.

As a result of this fiasco, Anthony May, QC, was appointed to report on the failure of the criminal process and trial. His criticism was directed at the tardiness of the investigators' report, the inexperience of both the Attorney General and the police in what was for them an unprecedented situation, the lack of communication between these parties, and the indecisiveness regarding whose responsibility it was to initiate proceedings. (Rodney Klevan QC, representing Norman Ashton-Hill, had

earlier remarked that World War II had been fought and won in the time
it took the authorities to decide whether or not to initiate criminal
proceedings). Among his conclusions Anthony May stated:

> ..the inspectors' report has not been published within a reasonable
> time of the events to which it relates. The inspection delayed the
> criminal investigation, and this, with other delays, resulted in the
> eventual prosecution being stayed. Even if the prosecution had not
> been stayed, it would still have been profoundly unsatisfactory for
> the trial to take place 5, 6, 7 or 8 years after the latest of the frauds
> with which it was concerned.[53]

Regarding the official lack of experience he had noted, he observed:
'it does not require detailed personal experience of fraud investigation to
discharge a general responsibility for seeing that serious crime is
effectively investigated and brought to court.'[54]

Finally, a civil action alleging negligence and breach of duty brought
against six members of the Finance Board and Treasurer Bill Dawson
personally (it being held that the Treasury had no legal personality and the
office of Treasurer was not a corporation sole) failed in 1986. A further
action was disallowed in April 1989 on the basis of a precedent provided
by a Privy Council decision on a similar matter in Hong Kong, which
ruled that officials owed no duty of care to depositors.[55]

It is said that there is no such thing as bad publicity; the SIB *débâcle*,
despite the deficiencies it revealed, did more than any advertisement or
road show to thrust the Isle of Man into the public consciousness as a
place providing financial services. Ironically, between 31st March 1982
and 31st March 1983, banking deposits rose at the unprecedented rate of
34.5%, from £1,074m to £1,445m. Despite the usual condescending
aspersions cast upon the Island by the ill-informed, more intelligent
people were well aware that malpractice and supervision failures occur
from time to time in the best-regulated financial environments, even in
the great City of London itself.

The Manx government was now fully aware that it urgently needed to
stabilise and control the monster of financial services which it had created.

CHAPTER 7

A NEW FOUNDATION

Lack of Supervision

Until the summer of 1982 the Manx Treasury proved quite incapable of exercising control over the burgeoning financial industry. This failure could not entirely be laid at the door of either the Treasurer or the Commercial Relations Officer; however, although they had at their disposal some tools of enforcement and a certain amount of information, they displayed little inclination to tackle even those problems of which they had, almost incidentally, become aware.

This inadequacy dates back to the time the Island's financial services were first established after the abolition of surtax, even before Bill Dawson took up the new position of Treasurer in October 1969. He immediately set about fulfilling the clear and urgent task entrusted to him by the Lieutenant Governor and the Finance Board, namely, the creation of a financial services industry in the Isle of Man. It does not appear to have occurred to anyone that, in order to ensure an orderly and reliable industry, it was necessary to put in place the appropriate controls. As far as banking was concerned, the Treasurer believed that the internal systems of the UK clearing banks' branches, and those of the first merchant bank subsidiaries, would constitute an adequate substitute for external controls; this attitude was encouraged by the banks themselves. But the new independent private banks were a different matter altogether; here, external supervision was urgently needed, and there were those who appreciated this. Charles Cain, for example, who had recently returned to the Island to open the Slater Walker subsidiary, drew attention to the need for regulation.

In 1975, a Banking Act was introduced, which, although it was well drafted, did not go far enough in specifying the means by which they could control the industry, and it was the case that the notion of supervision found little favour either within the industry itself or with Government. In a memorandum dated 9th January 1974, Eric Heath, General Manager of the Isle of Man Bank, after a meeting between himself and the Finance Board relating to the proposed Banking Bill stated that, after long and earnest consideration of Section 5, he had pointed out that the commercial banks were subject to audit by qualified firms of Chartered Accountants, and that there would not appear to be a need for further auditing by the Manx Government's Finance Department.[56]

Another memorandum of a meeting held on 8th August 1979 between the Chairman of the Finance Board, Percy Radcliffe, Board members Major Geoffrey Crellin and Edward Kermeen, and the Treasurer, recorded that the latter, when asked by Kermeen whether he was satisfied that the Island's small banking operations were being conducted on a sound basis, replied that the Treasury were unable to control the private banks without the introduction of banking inspection. The Treasurer added that private banks were often controlled by a small number of shareholders who might be less interested in observing sound banking principles than in generating greater personal profit. Moreover in many cases the private banks did not have the same standards of internal controls on loan policy as the larger organisations did, nor did they have internal inspection systems or internal audit. Under the existing self-regulation system problems could arise in a small bank of which the Treasury might be unaware. In sum, any problems that did arise within the banking sector were likely to concern private banks because of their small size and lack of reserves. The Treasurer conceded that whereas private banks might be able to provide services not catered for by the larger organisations, and the development of the business of small banks might offer short-term advantages, these advantages could well be outweighed by the potential long-term disadvantages arising from weak management structures; the Finance Board should be under no illusion as to the risks. Moreover, without banking inspection there was no way of assessing a bank's true financial position. In the face of these reservations, the majority of Board members nevertheless indicated that they were not in favour of employing inspectors; there would, after all, have been a cost to this.

In the same memorandum the Commercial Relations Officer stated that he favoured encouraging a money-broking operation in the Island. On the question of bank examination, he supported the Treasurer's view that inspection of the smaller banking institutions was essential in order to ensure that business was being conducted on prudent lines. Asked by the Chairman if he himself would be able to 'keep an eye on things', the CRO replied that he could certainly do that, but pointed out that this would only mean a superficial supervision; in no way could it be regarded as equivalent to banking inspection.

Notwithstanding these reservations the Board decided that they were content with the CRO 'keeping an eye on things', and decided against the introduction of a system of banking inspection.

In conclusion, when the Treasurer sought an indication from the Finance Board on the policy to be adopted towards new applications for licences from independent financial institutions, he was told that it was interested in expanding the financial sector and that small institutions should not be discouraged.

Thus, despite the Treasurer's reservations regarding his ability to control private banks without banking inspection, and the Commercial Relations Officer's reservations regarding 'keeping an eye on things' as an effective method of supervision, the Board declared themselves in favour of the expansion of the financial sector, and rejected the notion of banking supervision. The outcome was that supervision, such as it was, was left to the CRO, Peter Duncan, who had worked for the Treasury for some eight years. The Treasurer, Bill Dawson, stated, in an interview on 13th August 1999, that 'he [Duncan] was the first point of call. If he didn't provide information it wouldn't come from anyone else. If there were problems I would have expected him to have come along'.[57]

The problem arose when the 'first point of call' failed in its function. There is some indication that this is what happened at the time of the SIB collapse. Dawson claimed that the summaries of the quarterly reports, where all information contained in the banks' reports was collated, had not been forthcoming for six months. Certainly, the necessary action was

AIB building in Finch Road, Douglas. The planners thought that the new office for the Allied Irish Bank echoed the existing elegant houses, now offices, along Finch Road. It did, but not in scale.

not taken. The Chadwick Report states:

> Supervision and monitoring require a comparison of current and past data in order to identify norms and trends. We would have expected this to be self-evident to Duncan, who had qualified as a chartered accountant and who had had experience in industry. Duncan has declined to tell us whether there was some system within Treasury for the analysis and comparison of quarterly returns. As we have said, we have seen no documents evidencing such a system. If there was, in fact, no system of this nature, then it appears to us that the Finance Board was, in practice, quite unable to carry out the task of supervision which it had been set under the Banking Act. [58]

After the general election of 1981 Dr Edgar Mann had taken over as Chairman of the Finance Board. Even after twenty years of the New

Residents policy, Dr Mann inherited Government reserves of only one and a half million pounds, and an economy in evident decline. The new Chairman set about attracting new residents and new banks. However, he was unable to persuade the Executive Council, one of whose members, Ian Anderson, was a director of the Isle of Man Bank, to support the appointment of a proper banking supervisor, on the grounds that this would entail extra costs for major commercial banks which already had properly functioning internal control systems in place. This echoed the sentiment expressed by the bank's General Manager, Eric Heath, back in 1974. Dr Mann, with considerable foresight, warned the Executive Council: 'You may well rue this day'.

This was how matters stood when R. H. Farrant and W. M. Hyde compiled their *Report on Banking Supervision in the Isle of Man,* which they presented to the Government in December 1982 (although it was not published until May 1990). Farrant and Hyde were critical of the way the Banking Act 1975 had operated in practice, both in respect of the issuing of licences and of supervision, both for banking licences and financial advertising licences. Of the latter, the report states:

> The Treasurer is badly placed under the Act to supervise the holders of financial advertising licences. Indeed it would seem that the authors of the Act did not really envisage their supervision. The Treasurer has no powers to make requests or recommendations or to issue directions, or make inspections. [59]
>
> It seems to us that financial advertising licences have been available virtually on demand.

On the subject of banking licences, it states:

> This open-handed policy, together with inadequate research on the persons associated with applications, has meant that undesirables could all too easily obtain authority to take deposits or to manage other people's money.[60]
>
> This is surprising, for to judge from public statements made about the time the Banking Act was introduced the intention then was for a small number of banks of high quality and reputation, rather than a large number of banks, some of them of unknown quality and without reputation. The implication was that applications for

*HSBC building, Douglas. This hotch potch of bolted-on ornament replaced an
unattractive motley of buildings at the top of Victoria Street.
It now houses HSBC and the Insurance and Pensions Authority.*

banking licences would have to meet exacting criteria. In practice,
the criteria have not been exacting at all; persons with limited
banking experience have been awarded licences without even having
to propose to offer a banking business as defined in the Act.[61]
In our view it is.... likely that the Treasury did not appreciate how
loose was its vetting of new applications for banking licences and
the criteria applied to them, in spite of the warnings which were
made both by banks in the Isle of Man and by an overseas
supervisory authority.[62]

Of the quarterly reporting system and monitoring, the report concludes:
Its usefulness for supervision is very limited and perhaps for that

reason the Treasury has paid little regard to it. It has some value in assessing liquidity…However, there is no analysis of the maturity of deposits or of loans and investments. It is of no use at all in assessing capital adequacy, for the capital is not reported, and it is not possible to deduce it from the information that is reported. It is also of no use in assessing open positions in foreign exchange.[63]

We believe this cavalier attitude has been encouraged by the impression of muddle and inefficiency which the Treasury has presented to the outside world in its dealings with licence holders. This has been caused by inadequate clerical and secretarial backup. Requests for information or for action were often not followed up. Incoming letters were often not acknowledged. This impression has been in contrast to the impression of efficiency which has been fostered when dealing with new applicants, to a degree that the attitude has developed in the market place that the Treasury is more interested in attracting new business than policing what is already here.[64]

As Chief Minister Miles Walker was to concede several years later, on 22nd May 1990, in an interview with the *Isle of Man Examiner* newspaper:

The [Farrant] report does not point out some marginal deficiency. It condemns the system of the day, root and branch, and it is difficult, looking back from the comprehensive and sophisticated regulatory system of today, to recognise the situation described in the report.

Grasping the Nettle

Some steps had already been taken towards improving the situation. In September 1982 Dr Martin Owen was appointed as Commercial Relations Officer, replacing Peter Duncan, who had resigned in May 1982. Earlier in 1982 the part-time post of banking supervisor had been advertised at a salary of £100 per week; by August the position had been re-advertised at £25,000 per annum. Even this level of pay was outside the salary range approved by the Civil Service Commission; to circumvent this limitation, and to act with the urgency that was required, the Treasury hired the new banking and insurance supervisors on direct contracts. Jim Noakes, an experienced banking supervisor, and Duncan Neil, who had wide experience in the commercial insurance industry, took up their posts on 1st January 1983. The Financial Supervision Commission (FSC) was established by order in June 1983, with Martin Owen as administrator, the two supervisors as members, and Dr Edgar Mann, Chairman of the Finance Board, as Chairman, assisted by Rory Watson QC, a distinguished Chancery silk, and Lionel Bell, a retired bank manager. When Martin Owen resigned to take up a position with the Isle of Man Bank, Mark Solly, who had previously been the Island's Assessor of Income Tax, was appointed on 14th February 1984 as Director of the FSC. Solly's position was anomalous in that, although ostensibly in charge of operations, he himself was not a member of the Commission, whereas his subordinate supervisors were. The Commission was accommodated in shabby premises in Finch Road in Douglas, sharing a single secretary. Tynwald was nervous about the new appointments, and instructed three leading figures from banking, insurance and the corporate sector to keep an eye on the FSC's activities.

In some respects, the enterprise was doomed from the outset. The personalities of the three FSC officials were never in harmony. Duncan Neil, the Insurance Supervisor, had had a career working for large insurance companies; he had wide experience of the industry including the generation of new business. He perceived himself as fulfilling a dual role, both that of attracting new insurance companies to the Island, and that of regulating the activities of existing insurance companies, in spite of the inherent conflict between these two activities. Despite the delicacy of this position he apparently encountered no serious problems in the regulation of the industry. If problems there were, they were dealt with discreetly. The same applied to Dr William Hastings, Neil's successor after his retirement, and David Vick, who in turn succeeded Dr Hastings in 2005. All three men were approachable and ready to listen to new ideas, for instance, that of the protected cell company, which was set up in Duncan Neil's day, but never in fact used then.

Jim Noakes, on the other hand, came from a long career in banking supervision, with the Bank of England during the secondary banking crisis, with the Kuwait Investment Office, and in Bahrain, whence he came to the Island. A man of severe, even puritanical, disposition he did

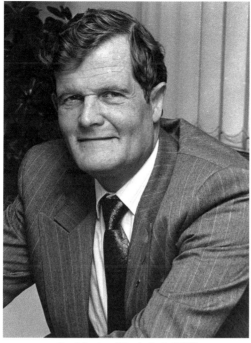

Jim Noakes, Head of the FSC.

not appear to welcome ideas from practitioners with an open mind. This obduracy is exemplified by his determined opposition, along with Mark Solly, to proposals made around 1986 by a group of leading and reputable practitioners from the field of trust and company administration. In a discussion paper drafted by Charles Cain, this group expressed concern about the poor quality of work being carried out by some members of the sector. The group feared that, even if, as the Commission and Attorney General asserted, Manx company law was sufficiently powerful to deal with misuse of Manx companies, the use, by Island-based practitioners, of companies and trusts of other jurisdictions could, if such enterprises were badly or dishonestly administered, tarnish the Island's reputation irrevocably, especially in the wake of the damage inflicted by the SIB collapse. Jurisdictions such as Panama, Liberia or Turks and Caicos were popular; in some of these jurisdictions, where regulation existed at all, it was minimal.

David Cannan, MHK. Treasury Minister 1986-89.

The group's proposals were rejected, and the proposers threatened with a defamation action; possibly this reaction sprang from a fear of disrupting this profitable sector, with unforeseeable consequences and subsequent loss of business. Ironically, the group's proposals were almost identical with the regulations eventually introduced in the Corporate and Trust Service Providers legislation in 2000[65], and again in 2005.

Jim Noakes made a revelatory remark to the Chamber of Commerce around 1988; using the simile of a sewerage operation, he said that his task as banking supervisor was to 'keep the water bathable, rather than potable'.[66] Those working in the finance industry had already sensed an attitude of hostility and disapproval, and this perception was reinforced by David Cannan, MHK, Treasury Minister under Miles Walker, who made repeated reference to what he called 'the grubby end of the market'. The conflict between the two supervisors' different perceptions of their function, Duncan Neil embracing the role of developer, Jim Noakes that

Mark Solly, Assessor of Income Tax and subsequently Head of the FSC.

of inquisitor, culminated in a split in 1984; a new Insurance Authority, independent of the FSC, was created, which expanded in 1996 into an Insurance and Pensions Authority. By 2007 it had a staff of twelve.

The dual regime of Noakes and Solly was continually embroiled in conflict; partly because of their personalities, and partly because of the unclear lines of responsibility. However, after consideration by the non-executive members of the FSC, Solly was induced to resign by the banking supervisor, his notional subordinate, and by the Treasury Minister, David Cannan. Thereafter, Jim Noakes ran the FSC efficiently if severely until his own retirement in 1998. Ironically, and perhaps surprisingly for one so critical of such manoeuvres in others, well before his retirement Noakes had made arrangements to join the board of the Isle of Man Bank, one of the most important of his charges.

It has to be said that there was justification for the control of financial services both in banking and generally, and that abuses in the field of

Coutts building, Onchan. Designed by Ellis Brown in country house style to impress the superior customers of Coutts. It has been converted into apartments.

insurance were few if any and that therefore a different approach was appropriate. However, despite the reluctance to tackle abuses in the field of companies and trusts just referred to, there was general and often expressed official disapproval of practitioners in financial services which appeared even to the most meticulous and scrupulous to include them too. The sewerage simile is a vivid example; another, in a speech by Jim Noakes to the Institute of Bankers on 10th March 1993 refers to the 'abuse of it [confidentiality] by clients and the *so-called professionals* who advise them.' He goes on 'It is not surprising perhaps that those same so-called professionals are anxious to throw the blame on the FSC, or the Attorney General'. Returning to his speech to the Isle of Man Chamber of Commerce he says 'Throughout the years of the Commission's life the tom-tom of over-regulation has continued to be beaten by those who are afraid. This fear seems to have two main sources and the simplest and most graphical way of describing them is to return to the Douglas baths. Some people in the finance sector...seem to be afraid that the Commission will either put too much chlorine in the water and deter bathers, or that somehow the Commission's careless big toe will pull out the plug and empty the bath altogether.' (The metaphor has got a bit mixed here from swimming baths.) He does go on to say that he does 'not regard them [these views] as held by the majority', and that the Island 'must (as Deemster Corrin suggests) tackle the area of company administrators and trustees and the abuse of Manx companies.' In a paper on the abuse of Manx companies, commissioned by the Manx government, Deemster Corrin concentrated his proposals on reforming Manx company law; but the proposal to deal with company administrators and trustees had been made to the FSC, and rejected, not long before, as just described.

Again he returns to the moral theme in a talk to tax accountants given on 16th April 1994.[66] He defines the black economy in the widest terms, covering illegal immigration, slavery, sweatshops...and moonlighting at one end, through counterfeiting, commercial piracy, industrial espionage...to bribery, corruption, illegal arms dealing and sanctions busting at the other. 'Essentially, the black economy is an evasion industry...[depending] crucially on secrecy, or its more polite alternative, confidentiality.' He continues: 'As practising tax accountants, you will be more aware than I am of the difficult practical and moral choices that face you. At least you will if you care about professional status. One of the sad things that has happened in the last 20 years has been the decline in public estimation of the professions. At least I think it is sad, because professional ethics have always seemed to me one of the bulwarks of society. Over the years they have been undermined by the activity of a minority of 'cowboy professionals', who have effectively prostituted their professional status.'

The 'sad' thing (to use a favourite word) is that professionals in the Island were likely to believe that all were included in these strictures, and, despite his disclaimers, that coloured their perception of him and the FSC as a whole, with its ever growing scope. Nevertheless much was achieved beyond sorting out the acute banking problems inherited in 1983, many of them pioneering, ahead of measures which would inevitably be imposed. Among these, as he said to the Chamber of Commerce in 1991, 'the Isle of Man was the first offshore jurisdiction:

- to advise and implement a Know Your Customer policy against money laundering (1985)

- to obtain designated territory status from the UK under the Financial Services Act (1988)
- to devise and implement a regulatory framework for non-UK marketable collective investment schemes, the so-called restricted schemes (1990)
- to introduce a depositors' compensation scheme (Feb 1991)'.[66]

After the SIB collapse the first action of the new FSC in March 1983 was to impose a moratorium on the issuing of new bank licences and undertake a critical review of licences currently in operation, especially those of local banks which did not have banking parents. A new banking code of practice had been introduced in September 1982, which included the requirement to disclose major loans. This resulted in the suspension of International Mercantile Finance (IMF), when it was required to increase its paid up share capital from £2 to £100,000. It had earlier accepted as a deposit £2m, part of the proceeds of the Brinksmat robbery, apparently without demur. When Chancellor Finance produced its quarterly returns for 31st March 1983, incomplete and two weeks late, the Treasurer ordered Chancellor to place all new deposits into a separate trust account. Kingsnorth Bank's directors re-domiciled the bank outside the new regime, to Anguilla, where shortly afterwards it went into liquidation. This purge of weak and inappropriate banking institutions, many of which were used as a source of cheap finance so that their owners could carry out other activities, was carried out with very little disturbance as far as the public was aware; it was a master-class in discreet supervisory management even if there were occasional shouting matches over the boardroom table between the Supervisor and Directors as closures were enforced.

But the biggest challenge was to come on 5th July 1990 when the Bank of Credit and Commerce International SA failed world-wide. BCCI had established a branch in the Island in 1979; this branch had not yet been made a subsidiary which might have provided greater security for Island depositors. As it was the depositors with the Isle of Man branch were subsumed into the bank's general creditors world-wide. The failure of BCCI, which was brought about at least in part by systematic fraud,

BCCI building, Douglas. Formerly Martins and Barclays banks.

was attributed to a lack of effective supervision between jurisdictions. Although the bank was incorporated in Luxemburg much of its business was conducted through London, and the Bank of England was blamed for failing to identify and prevent the problem. However, the effect of the collapse on depositors with the Manx branch was cushioned by the depositors' compensation scheme, set up for depositors with Island banks, which came into effect from 1st February 1991; under this the Island's Treasury, using the powers conferred by Section 21 of the Financial Supervision Act 1988, could require licensed banks to contribute pro rata to the compensation fund to provide 75% of up to £20,000 for each depositor. The compensation could be paid without delay, well in advance of the conclusion of the liquidation. The contributing banks became general creditors for the amounts contributed,

Bank of Ireland building, Douglas. Built for the Investment Bank of Ireland in the style of their Dublin offices, it unfortunately seems to have acquired the elements of its porch from a job lot of garden furniture.

and, in this case, in due course virtually the whole amount was recovered. At all events, the scheme proved effective in forestalling the kind of public outcry produced by the SIB collapse nine years earlier.

It may well have been the BCCI calamity which occasioned David Cannan's removal from his post as Treasury Minister. In the summer of 1989, when rumours of the BCCI's problems first began to circulate, Bill Dawson as Treasurer asked Cannan to authorise the withdrawal from BCCI of the Government deposits which had been spread around between the Island's banks, both for security and by way of encouragement. This was an obvious and prudent step intended to safeguard Manx taxpayers' assets. Jim Noakes, however, objected that the Treasurer's action was open to criticism, since it was in conflict with his responsibilities as the Chairman of the FSC. After much deliberation the

Sir Miles Walker, MHK.

directors of the BCCI were informed that their licence would only be renewed on 1st January 1990 subject to their fulfilling three conditions: firstly, that the branch be incorporated; secondly, that the minimum capital should equal the Manx deposits; thirdly, that the Manx deposits should be ring-fenced by being deposited with institutions other than BCCI. In this way Manx depositors would be protected in the event that the parent bank ran into difficulties.

BCCI, both at local and London level, found these conditions unacceptable, and arranged for one of their senior directors to come to the Island to meet the Chief Minister, Miles Walker, and Jim Noakes. According to David Cannan, this meeting was to take place without his presence; he was not even informed. The senior director demanded and, in Cannan's view obtained, that the conditions for the renewal of the licence should be waived and that Cannan himself should be removed from office. In November 1989 Cannan was replaced as Treasury

The Royal Bank of Scotland, Loch Promenade, Douglas. Another example of a very clever planning application; the drawing made it appear to reflect the Victorian bays of Loch Promenade. The actuality is starkly modern. The adjacent empty spaces do nothing for Douglas.

Minister by Donald Gelling who restored the BCCI's licence without fulfilment of the three original conditions which would have protected the Island from the worst of the effects of the bank's subsequent collapse.

The reason Miles Walker gave for the removal of David Cannan as Treasury Minister was that Cannan was becoming increasingly unacceptable to members of Tynwald, and would be unlikely to be confirmed in office in the confirmation process for the ministerial team prescribed after three years of an administration. He therefore asked both Cannan and Dominic Delaney MHK, who was, in his opinion, in a similar position, to stand down. Walker repudiated the notion that Cannan's successful thwarting of the Chief Minister's proposal to construct a swimming pool at the Villa Marina on Douglas promenade was a factor.

Neither Cannan nor Delaney ever forgave Miles Walker; they went on to form the Alternative Policy Group, later changed to Action for Progressive Government, both conveniently shortened to APG, with Edgar Mann, Edgar Quine and Adrian Duggan. The APG functioned as an organised opposition, although on many issues there was common ground with the Government; in 1993 Mann and Duggan accepted membership of the Departments of Industry and Home Affairs, thus relinquishing a strictly opposition role.

The FSC proceeded to regulate financial services, other than insurance, systematically and with vigour, and its staff increased in numbers accordingly, from 7 in 1984 to 23 by 1998 and 63 by 2007. The Chairman of the Commission is no longer a Member of Tynwald, although the Chairman and non-executive Commissioners are appointed by Tynwald. There are inevitably potential conflicts of interest, since experience within the industry is highly desirable for those holding such posts, yet at the same time those who possess such experience tend to be former or current employees of supervised entities.

Apart from Celtic Bank, there are no longer any privately owned banks in the Island; changes of ownership require the Commission's prior consent. A small mutual savings bank, the Isle of Man Bank for Savings, which had existed without any trouble since 1834, had to close in 1988 for various reasons: it did not comply with the new model, had suffered some fraud, and was too small. On the other hand, Conister Trust, founded as a public company in 1935 and which took deposits for the purposes of hire purchase and other loan finance, converted to a full banking licence in 1989, and in 2007 changed its name to Conister Finance.

New Laws for New Problems

New legislation was gradually introduced to supplement the Banking Act 1975 and replace the Prevention of Frauds (Investments) Act of 1965. An Insurance Act was passed in 1986 setting out the powers of the new Insurance Authority. For the FSC, the Financial Supervision Act

1988 set out the constitution and powers of the Commission to include regulation of collective investment schemes, banking business, building societies, and to provide for the establishment of compensation schemes. This was to some degree a response to the UK Financial Services Act 1986; it dealt in particular with the control of investment business and represented a pioneering piece of legislation on the part of the Island which was to serve as a model for the legislation of other similar jurisdictions. Its functions have been extended to assume most of the duties of the Companies Registry, and the regulation and supervision of corporate and trust service providers.

Certain criteria and methods have been established for the regulation of the financial services activities included in the new legislation. Any regulated business is required to be owned and managed by 'fit and proper' persons. All business must be controlled by at least 'four eyes', that is to say, by at least two suitably qualified or experienced, responsible persons. The information to be included on quarterly banking returns is specified; it must show, for example, capital adequacy, liquidity, maturity of deposits and advances, large loans above a proportion of the free capital of the bank, &c. Officials of the FSC are required to visit licence holders at least once a year: all this is in accordance with good banking practice. The FSC was also the first body to encourage the 'know your customer' philosophy, long before money-laundering and compliance procedures were introduced in an effort to eradicate crime, initially largely drugs-related, but increasingly, especially since 11th September 2001, related to international terrorist networks; these procedures were introduced in the Isle of Man under The Prevention of Terrorism Act 1990.

Previously clients had been regularly accepted without undue investigation of their backgrounds and bona fides, structures had been set up without recording their true purpose, and deposits were accepted by banks often without enquiry as to the provenance of funds. There were frequent reports of suitcases of cash being presented at the counters of local banks for deposit. There is little doubt that the purposes included blatant tax evasion, and safe keeping of funds derived from or intended for criminal purposes, including money from both sides of the conflict in

Northern Ireland for whom the Island presented a handy, and ofte
actually visible, haven.

The collapse of the SIB trial saw the introduction of the Criminal
Justice Act 1990 which spelled out the power of the Attorney General to
authorize investigation of potential fraud, with reciprocal arrangements
with the Serious Fraud Office in London and Edinburgh. A fraud squad
had been introduced in the Island in 1987, but lack of experience,
particularly in the light of the intermittent need for their employment, set
them at a disadvantage. It was claimed that much of their time was spent
on traffic policing.

The supervisory powers of the FSC have been further defined in the
Investment Business Act 1991 and Banking Act 1998 and the Corporate
Service Providers Act 2000, which was extended by the Fiduciary Services
Act 2005 to cover provision of trustee services by professionals. Finally,
under the Criminal Justice (Money Laundering Offences) Act 1998, a new
criminal principle was introduced; in the case of evasion of the taxes of
other jurisdictions, it had always been the convention that the authorities
of one jurisdiction took no part in enforcing the taxation of another.
However, pressure from the United States and those states in the
European Union which had less sophisticated anti-avoidance legislation,
and tolerated such simple evasion tactics as concealing gold Napoleons
under rural mattresses (in France) or placing money in bank accounts in
neighbouring countries (long practised in Germany, Ireland, Italy and
Greece) forced two new developments. The criminalisation of assisting in
tax evasion now means that professional tax lawyers and accountants run
the risk of personal prosecution leading to imprisonment. The risk also
extends to those who offer professional advice on tax schemes presumed
to be legal but which may be in the event be ruled to be illegal.[67]

In addition the arrangements for reporting bank interest earned on
deposits in one jurisdiction to the tax authorities of the beneficial owner
in another, have been designed to discourage undeclared offshore
deposits and to tap into hitherto untaxed revenue. However, certain
countries including Switzerland, Luxembourg, Channel Islands and the
Isle of Man negotiated the alternative of not reporting individual interest

to the relevant tax authorities, but instead deducting tax on a progressive scale, initially at 15% (in effect a withholding tax); half of this tax is to be paid in a lump sum to the various countries of residence. Although it was believed that this would result in a drop in offshore deposits, in practice there has been little noticeable change in the situation, perhaps because the new arrangement was confined to bank interest only and did not affect other forms of income such as dividends.

These attacks on offshore financial centres by the USA and EU featured black lists of offending jurisdictions, compiled on the basis of general prejudice and distrust, with very little foundation. The Isle of Man initially appeared on the black list, but was removed after representations and after a report produced by Andrew Edwards in 1998 at the instigation of the UK Home Office. According to the former Chief Minister, Donald Gelling, this report was commissioned not as an attack on the Isle of Man, but rather to give the then Chancellor of the Exchequer, Gordon Brown, the evidence of an independent report which gave the Isle of Man a clean bill of health and which he could use to rebuff external criticism. Entitled *A Review of Financial Regulation in the Crown Dependencies* this report covered the Isle of Man, Jersey and Guernsey. A similar review was prepared by KPMG with particular reference to Gibraltar, Bermuda, Virgin Islands, Turks and Caicos Islands and Cayman Islands, as a consequence of which all these jurisdictions were removed from the black list. In the case of the Isle of Man the Edwards report commented on all the matters already described in this chapter, mentioned areas where improvements were in preparation, and displayed an appreciation of the efforts that the Isle of Man and the Channel Islands had devoted to the development of a structure of legislation and supervision. The changes which had taken place in the sixteen years since 1982 had been remarkable, and all three jurisdictions emerged from the review with flying colours as highly reputable financial centres, sloughing off the pejorative epithets of 'tax haven' and 'offshore'. They are indeed small, independent jurisdictions with low taxation: this category includes jurisdictions that are firmly onshore, like Switzerland, Luxembourg, Liechtenstein and Monaco; in addition there are low tax jurisdictions among member countries of the EU, particularly the new countries of Eastern Europe, Cyprus, Malta, and parts of Ireland. In his conclusion, Edwards stated: 'I have no doubt that the Islands are in the top division of offshore centres'.[68]

However, the progress reflected in these results, attained by means of legislation and regulation, has not been achieved without much criticism and at substantial cost. It might be argued that the costs involved in regulating such areas as financial supervision, money laundering, health and safety, gender, race, disability and age discrimination and so on are an inevitable fact of modern life. It might even be argued that the pendulum has swung too far the other way, to a point where cumbersome bureaucratic procedures now threaten to destroy the very aspects of life they are designed to regulate, and that the more robust traditional approach, summed up in the expression *caveat emptor*, though it had its casualties, was preferable. Certainly, despite the improvements precipitated by the collapse of SIB, the Isle of Man has come under increasing external pressure from the EU, USA, OECD, Financial Action Task Force and other bodies to comply with all manner of rules and regulations. It sometimes appears as though the EU no sooner detects financial success than it seeks to suppress it through the imposition of bureaucratic and often unnecessary intervention. Although the British Government would probably not initiate such measures of its own accord, it is the channel through which such pressure is applied, and this despite the fact that the success of the financial industries on the islands also benefits the financial resources and increases the wealth of the City of London and the United Kingdom as a whole.

It is, perhaps, inevitable that supervision should grow increasingly heavy handed. In the first place, politicians wish to protect their own and the Island's reputation. The burden is passed on to the Financial Supervision Commission (or Insurance and Pensions Authority) who share this aim; FSC officials entrusted with the task devise procedures that are probably more intrusive and bureaucratic than they really need to be. Those who administer the detailed paperwork or inspections are the least experienced and possibly the least qualified to decide precisely what is required. On the other hand, the supervised institution, for example a bank, is so nervous of inviting any criticism which might affect its reputation with the FSC that it draws up manuals of procedure that are even more bureaucratic. The operation of the manuals governing such activities as opening a bank account is placed in the hands of relatively junior clerks, too inexperienced to dare to interpret the manuals except in the narrowest way possible. Common sense flies out the window; for example, there is a requirement to 'know your client', commonly accomplished by means of a passport and photograph, a utility bill to confirm the address, and some sort of statement to show the source of funds. These items are routinely and without thought placed on file. In the case of total strangers, they may be the best evidence available, but of themselves they prove nothing. Demanding such documentation from long-standing customers can be perceived as insulting, especially to customers who have already dealt with the bank, often for many years, or with a subsidiary which already holds the 'know your client' information on file and could easily share it within the group, for example between Barclays and Barclays Finance. Likewise, various FSC members and officials have indicated that, particularly in the case of long-standing Island residents, besides the transference of confirmation between members of a group, a note in the file confirming knowledge of a client for many years would constitute acceptable 'know your client' documentation. But there is a climate of fear; unfortunately common sense appears unlikely to prevail at any stage in the process.

If the Isle of Man could find a way of replacing the present ponderous machinery with refined procedures involving minimum supervision and documentation, it might well steal a march on its competitors once again.

CHAPTER 8

TAX HAVEN OR FINANCIAL CENTRE?

Taxation Background

In 1935, in a case heard in the House of Lords involving payments by the Duke of Westminster to some of his staff, Lord Tomlin uttered the famous dictum: 'Every man is entitled if he can to order his affairs so that the tax attaching under the appropriate Acts is less than it otherwise would be'. This chapter should be read in the light of this observation: it confirms what was believed to be the legal basis of tax planning.

It is necessary to distinguish between avoidance and tax evasion. Tax avoidance involves using existing tax laws and treaties in order to reduce, quite legally, the tax liabilities of a person or company. It often involves expert tax planning to provide the appropriate structures or arrangements. It can, however, be very simple: for example getting married carries a number of tax benefits not available to two separate, even if co-habiting, individuals. Tax evasion, on the other hand, involves concealing income or assets from a tax authority which has a legal right to exact taxation on them, either simply (for example under the mattress) or by using structures, such as companies or trusts, and by using nominee names which actually have no legal effect for tax purposes, but serve to hide the income or assets from the legitimate authority. The use of numbered bank accounts in Switzerland or Liechtenstein was a traditional method used on the Continent, though recently brought to light. In recent years, governments have sought to reclassify legitimate avoidance as tantamount to evasion.

The Isle of Man was widely used as a base for evasion in the bad old days of the 1970s, as well as for proper tax planning. Tax evasion was held to be a matter solely for the taxing authority, not for the authorities of the places used for concealment and although illegal was not always regarded as criminal. However, with the new emphasis on 'know your client' and

Heritage Court, Douglas. The least aptly named building in the Island. Dull, ugly and not even utilitarian. It had three doors and three sets of awkward steps and three staircases. It is now wholly occupied by KPMG. One of several contributions by Roy Kermode and Bryan Stott.

money-laundering, tax evasion has been reclassified as a criminal activity.

A tax planning scheme, deemed by the courts to be unsuccessful, now can have the effect that the creators of the scheme may be in danger of criminal prosecution. The result of this reclassification has been to very much focus the minds of those who previously were devising inventive and elaborate schemes without fear of personal liability.

Certainly the game that was played between tax professionals and the Commissioners of Inland Revenue was, until about 1990, relatively gentlemanly. Although those who blatantly cheated were seriously pursued and penalized, tax professionals, even those who devised artful tax-planning procedures which remained within the letter of the law, were treated as fellow practitioners in tax law rather than as criminals involved in a conspiracy to evade UK taxes; sparring between the parties was conducted within sensible bounds. Although taken seriously, it might be thought of as a typically English game.

Two things have occurred to change this culture: the first of these events was the appointment as Chancellor of a puritanical Scottish Presbyterian, a son of the manse, whose apparent loathing of tax-payers led him to devise strategies for extorting ever greater amounts of tax revenue in order to finance his increasingly ineffectual revenue extravagance (laughingly described as 'investment'). To aid him in his depredations the Inland Revenue was amalgamated with Customs and Excise to form the new department of HM Revenue and Customs. Customs and Excise wields massive and arbitrary powers, appropriate for dealing with those who break the law, for example, by smuggling; the department possesses the power to seize goods, invade premises, even private homes, at any hour of the day or night, and to bear arms. These powers all date back several hundred years. The traditional powers of the Inland Revenue, on the other hand, were largely documentation and office-based; their strength lay in the letter of the law rather than in the exercise of force. The amalgamation of these two departments means that the resultant department's culture relies more on force than on the application of the law alone.

The second factor affecting the development of this more punitive culture is the pursuit, by supranational bodies such as the European Union, OECD, and United States Revenue, of greater power in respect of tax evasion, which is treated as a criminal activity on a par with drug-trafficking and terrorism, especially that associated with Al Qaeda. (Terrorism associated with Ireland was always regarded more benignly, especially by the United States, the principal source of their funds). The long-established convention whereby no jurisdiction assisted in the identification and collection of the tax revenues of another jurisdiction is a thing of the past. Tax professionals can be treated as criminals if their tax-planning is held to be ineffective, or if their clients' returns, which they process and forward, are held to be wrong and therefore fraudulent. None of these developments is helpful; they obstruct the work of tax professionals to the detriment not only of them and tax-payers, but also of the Revenue department, in that they inhibit an open exchange of views and information.

The United States, the home of many of the malpractices has recently intensified its persecution of people both within the country and also outside its borders, who may have little to do with the United States. Ostensibly the justification offered for this extra-territorial interference is that the legislation is intended to deal with terrorism; however its inspiration owes much to the failures of the US system itself, such as the Enron scandal, or to the pet aversions of the US authorities, as witnessed by the prosecution of KPMG tax partners. Special opprobrium is reserved for small jurisdictions perceived (with moralizing arrogance) to be 'tax havens' (an outmoded designation, in any case). The most recent effort is the 'Stop Tax Haven Abuse Act' (the terms themselves beg all sorts of unanswered questions) introduced into the Senate by Senators Levin and Coleman, supported by the newly elected President Barack Obama when still a Senator. One wonders whether the proposed strictures will be extended to embrace such major onshore 'offshore' centres as Singapore or Switzerland, or even Delaware and Vermont? The unfortunate Liechtenstein has incurred the wrath of Germany after a bank employee there sold lists of tax evaders to the German (and British) authorities and thereby revealed just how much money was being concealed.

The halcyon days before these changes occurred may from today's perspective appear to have been relatively trouble-free. However, there were certainly some who cheated by downright evasion, concealing income or assets from the revenue of many jurisdictions. In the case of the Isle of Man, particularly in the early days, from the 1970s to the mid-1980s, this could be achieved very simply, through bank deposits, even using real names, or by using companies to hold assets and collect income, often associated with rather dubious trusts. Undoubtedly there were accountants, lawyers and bankers who were complicit in these activities. Of course, such practices were not confined to the Isle of Man; they were common in the Channel Islands, including Sark, the Cayman Islands, Bahamas, Turks and Caicos, and above all, in the country which has been

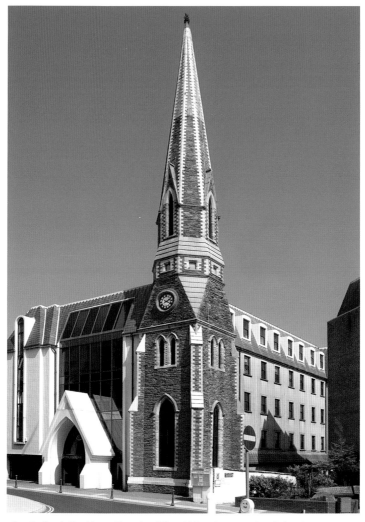

St Andrew's Buildings, Douglas. The old Presbyterian church has kept its tower and spire as a lift shaft.

the mother of all tax havens since time immemorial, Switzerland.

However, it has proved possible to take advantage of the Islands' status legitimately, too. Moralists may frown, but such activity is widespread and commonplace; major countries such as the USA, the United Kingdom and the Netherlands are involved in double tax

Friends Provident International, Arbory Road, Castletown.
Originally built for Sun Alliance International.

agreements which can provide legal tax shelters by treaty. If a jurisdiction is unhappy at the loss of revenue, it needs to introduce the appropriate preventative legislation which is why the tax laws of the United Kingdom run to many thousands of pages.

Let us examine the possibilities the Island offers to both individuals and corporations. Residence involves a place of abode with the characteristics of a settled home, i.e., a reasonable house or flat, not merely a *pied à terre*. The whole income of an individual resident in the Isle of Man will attract Manx tax, even if that individual is working abroad full-time.[69] But tax rates for residents, always low, have been further reduced. In 1987, David Cannan, as Treasury Minister, introduced a lower rate of 15% for the first band of income, with 20% as the standard and corporate rate, as well as transferable personal allowances. The nil rate band is substantial, as is the 10%, lower new rate, both are double for married couples, and the current standard rate of 18% is 2% lower than that of the Channel Islands. 24% of Manx personal incomes suffer no income tax at all, 39% reach the 10% band, and only some 37% reach the 18% level. In addition since 2006 there has been a cap of maximum tax payable of £100,000. People of substantial wealth, therefore, will never pay more than this sum, no matter how many millions they have. In 2007 this applied to 59 individuals. The money so paid goes directly to the Manx Treasury for the benefit of the Island, and from this point of view the system is advantageous. This, along with the creation of employment opportunities, constituted the prime motive behind the introduction of the New Residents policy in 1960.

To benefit from residency in the Island an individual must detach him or herself from the tax liability of other jurisdictions whose rules vary. The principal rule for the United Kingdom (and Ireland) is that the individual must not be physically present in those countries for more than 182 days in any year of assessment from 6th April to 5th April (in the UK) or for an average of more than 90 days over four years. Lack of an available accommodation in the UK has not been a requirement since 1993, although this may be helpful when demonstrating that an individual is genuinely resident in the Isle of Man and is no longer resident in the UK. Some Manx residents may sail close to the wind, either in respect of the number of days spent or the retention of substantial 'settled' accommodation, possibly laying them open to the accusation, levied by purists or nationalists, of being 'tax-dodgers'; but these are exceptions. The recent case of Robert Gaines-Cooper v HMRC (his residence in the Seychelles was held to be less real than that in the UK, both in respect of way of life and property, as well as days of presence) has sounded a note of caution.

A person not resident in the UK, but in the Isle of Man, should not be liable to UK Income Tax, apart from income arising in the UK such as pensions, dividends, rents or interest, nor to Capital Gains Tax except on the sale of trading assets in the UK. Individuals habitually resident in the Isle of Man may claim to have adopted a Manx domicile of choice, placing them beyond the reach of Inheritance Tax, except on UK assets (for example, property and shares) held by them in their own name. This

Royalty House, Douglas. A lively essay on an Art Deco theme on the site of the old white tiled Royalty cinema, now offices of Axa.

potential liability is easily eliminated by transferring such assets into, for example, a Manx private investment company, so that for Inheritance Tax purposes the nature of the assets becomes Manx property. The same procedure may also be used to shelter some forms of income. In this way a successful resident who becomes domiciled in the Island can be virtually free of UK Income Tax, Capital Gains Tax and Inheritance Tax; similar benefits may well be available for other jurisdictions.

The great advantage of a Manx domicile is that, so long as the domicile is protected by facts, a person may become resident in the United Kingdom and be taxable only on UK source income and remittances of income into the UK, and similarly with Capital Gains Tax. However, the UK Budget of 2008 introduced a tax charge of £30,000 for the continuance of this privilege. Likewise, the Island can be used with advantage as a place to keep assets, through a Manx or other company or otherwise, by persons whose domicile, birth or origin, lies elsewhere, for example, in the Republic of Ireland, the Middle-East, the Indian sub-continent, and many parts of Europe. Properly set up all these uses are perfectly legal and can provide legitimate sources of income to banks, corporate service providers, insurance companies and investment managers, ultimately benefiting the Island's economy. There may be those who disapprove, but this is one of the ways in which the Island earns its living, provides employment for its people and generates revenue for communal services.

Growth of Financial Services

In the corporate field the Island set out its stall to attract certain types of enterprise and business through its tax policies. Quite apart from the low taxes for individuals, which make the Island an inviting place for entrepreneurs and their employees to live, the Government has been at pains to frame its tax laws with a view to making the Island attractive as a location for financial business, and to compete successfully with other low-tax jurisdictions. In framing legislation calculated to enhance the Island's appeal for financial service providers, efforts have been made to prevent the abuse of its facilities by unscrupulous operators. It should be noted that any such tax privileges or enticements, with the notable exception of the overriding zero-rate for all companies, do not of themselves cost the Island any loss of revenue, since no revenue would arise if these companies had not been attracted in the first place. Many are well-known and highly reputable and their activities provide both employment and the resultant tax revenue. Those who are uncomfortable with these activities would do well to remember that, unlike grants to manufacturing or tourism, little Government expenditure has been devoted to the finance sector, apart from the cost of drafting the appropriate legislation and the recent provision, at long last, of a certain amount of support in the form of occasional publications, the appointment of a marketing manager, and the provision of an office in London for meetings. Many private firms based in the Island do no less.

Zurich International Life offices in Athol Street, Douglas.
An essay by Ellis Brown in an ornamental brick style.

After the introduction of the new regime of supervision and regulation put in place after the SIB collapse, growth resumed in both insurance and banking and in other areas. In the field of insurance, the growth in captive insurance numbers came to an end not only in the Island but throughout the 'captive' world; the decline started in 1999. However this has not meant a reduction of activity, since the size of many captives continued to grow in respect of the premiums and the funds they controlled, standing in 2006 at £1bn and £6½bn respectively. The UK captive market is mature and principally makes use of Guernsey and the Isle of Man, although locations within the EU, such as Dublin,

Luxemburg and Malta, which can take business direct without intermediaries, offer obvious advantages.

It is in the area of life assurance that the Isle of Man has been most successful, with 20 life companies by 2005, generating annual premiums of £9½bn and with £34bn under management, compared with two life companies in Guernsey and none at all in Jersey. The policies are largely savings schemes for expatriates, initially people from the UK working abroad, but now including Indians and Arabs in the Middle East, and nationals of Singapore, China and Korea in the Far East. The schemes share many of the characteristics of investment or unit trusts, and the £34bn under management needs to be considered alongside the more modest £7½bn in total managed in collective investment schemes. Most of the life companies involved are subsidiaries of major UK life companies or mutuals (that is, owned by their policy holders); in 2001, the sector employed 2,103 people, 55% of whom were women.

After the pause in issuing new banking licences, activity resumed strongly. The Island encouraged the establishment of building society subsidiaries. At first, this was limited to six of the major societies, after a change in UK legislation in 1986, under which building societies (which were mutuals,) were permitted to have subsidiaries. Since that time many of these building societies have been converted into limited companies on a par with regular banks, and have effectively become banks, some of them major quoted companies like Abbey National and Halifax, later merged with the Bank of Scotland. In addition some of the major banks established their head offices for international work in the Island; these included Barclays International, and Nat West Offshore (until it was taken over by the Royal Bank of Scotland). One of the principal reasons for this was the space the Island offered for expansion, especially after the announcement in March 1987 by both Jersey and Guernsey that no new businesses could be set up there, nor could existing businesses increase their staff numbers. Even though these announcements were retracted shortly afterwards they set alarm bells ringing in many institutions, causing them to react by setting up new parallel offices in the Island immediately, as did Rothschilds, or to expand their operation here, as did

Warburgs. These developments caused considerable expansion of business and resulted in a new surge of residents and increased house prices, both of which had for some years stagnated. By 2001, the banking sector employed some 3,130 people, 62% of them women. By 2005, bank deposits amounted to £37½bn, compared with £185bn in Jersey and £80bn in Guernsey; and by the middle of 2008 deposits stood at £54bn in 44 banks.

The one area in which the Isle of Man has been relatively unsuccessful is, ironically enough, the area in which it first provided financial services in 1963, that of fund management in the form of investment and unit trusts; between 1995 and 2005 the amount generated declined from just under £5bn to £2.8bn. All the growth in this area came from the less formal Experienced and Professional Investor funds which have grown over the same period from zero to £4.6bn; other categories now figuring in the statistics include overseas and international funds, and schemes totalling £8.9bn by the end of 2006, making a total of £16.5bn reported. By the middle of 2008 total funds under management had risen strongly to £57bn. This, of course, excludes the very considerable funds in the form of insurance policies already referred to.

However, very recently the Island has become a favoured jurisdiction to act as a base for companies launched on London's Alternative Investment Market. using the strong professional skills of advocates and accountants, fifteen of the top one hundred AIM companies are Manx incorporated, and 75% of all Indian AIM companies.

In the area of corporate taxes, no Isle of Man Income or Capital Gains Tax is assessable on the underlying investment or insurance funds, allowing policies or investments to accumulate untaxed. A series of exemptions was introduced for both categories, as well as for the interest on bank deposits in the Island. The management companies themselves were subject to Manx tax, but from 2006 the applicable rate for all companies resident or registered in the Isle of Man was reduced to nil, with the exception of banks, which pay 10% (which in most cases can be offset against the parent company's liability). This change was introduced principally in response to moralizing from Governments which objected that it was unfair that some companies in some jurisdictions could be exempted from paying tax while regular tax was levied on tax-resident companies. The Isle of Man, which had the good fortune, if not the foresight, to enjoy a strong revenue flow from indirect taxation (principally excise and VAT derived from the Customs and Excise Agreement with the UK) responded by simply making all companies of whatever description (except banks) liable at a common rate of nil. In so doing, the Island placed considerable pressure on other territories, especially the Channel Islands, where the revenue from indirect taxation is much less significant. But the Channel Islands have followed the Island's example and reduced corporate taxes, and have gone into government revenue deficit as a consequence. This clever move on the part of the Island will no doubt provoke a reaction from the 'bully' states in due course.

These advantageous tax concessions were formerly available to non-resident companies even in the UK and Ireland, but were withdrawn in those jurisdictions during the 1980s. In the Isle of Man, most non-resident companies were changed into companies exempt from Manx tax; but as a result of the reduction of the corporate rate to nil, the distinction no longer applies, since all companies, including insurance and shipping companies, are taxable equally at zero. Isle of Man resident shareholders remain liable for tax on their dividends.

The non-resident and Exempt companies have been the main vehicle, together with trusts, of the trust and corporate providers companies. In the early days not all the work was well executed or effective in law, but after the SIB fiasco matters began to improve. Quality was further improved by the Corporate Service Providers Act 2000, followed by the Fiduciary Services Act 2005, which forced some less satisfactory operators to pull out or to amalgamate. The official reluctance to take action against such operators fifteen years earlier, despite being urged to do so, may have been due to a fear of driving away businesses which supported employment and generated work, including for banks and investment managers. In fact the fallout was contained and in 2005 the sector provided some 1,500 jobs, half of these being filled by women.

Accountants and Advocates

After the collapse of SIB, the accounting firm of Peat Marwick Mitchell, as liquidator of the bank, greatly expanded its office which it had been on the point of closing in 1982. After amalgamating with J. G. Fargher & Co. to provide a local base, its strong expansion has continued. In 1989 Treasury Minister David Cannan awarded the Government audit to Peats (now KPMG). The audit had previously been conducted for over a century by Pannell Kerr Forster (and under its previous name of W. H. Walker & Co). The reason given was a wish for a change, although there was no obvious justification for it either on the grounds of quality or on cost. The nature of the exercise was changed, too, so that it became a purely passive audit rather than one that also helped the Government in the presentation of its accounts and with accounting problems; the consequences of this new approach became very evident when the finances of the Port St Mary Commissioners collapsed.

Of other accounting firms, Touche Ross, after an unsuccessful courtship of an old Manx firm, Shannon Kneale, set up independently and now practises as Deloitte. The relatively new firm of Breadner Moorhouse joined the international organization of Coopers and Lybrand, and now practises as PricewaterhouseCoopers; Shannon Kneale has joined the international firm of Ernst and Young. The professional services of all four firms are now based on audit, together with taxation and systems advice; their trust and company administration services were sold off as a consequence of pressures relating to possible conflicts of interest. The fear must be that, if financial services underwent a serious decline, the 'big four' would lose interest in the Island which would then revert to the position obtaining before 1982 with the locally owned firm of PKF as the sole surviving major firm on the ground. The Government might do well to bear this in mind when awarding its work, with a view to promoting and protecting local interests. The decision of David Cannan as Treasury Minister hardly set an encouraging precedent.[70]

During this same period the legal profession also underwent changes. The number of advocates rose steadily. Many advocates continued to work for small firms or as general practitioners, but a few of the larger firms began to introduce specialization, particularly in response to the growing volume of commercial work produced by the burgeoning financial sector. The two firms of Cains and Dickinson Cruickshank specialized and expanded, going on to become very large firms. The Island's courts and Deemsters were also under pressure, being required to deal with not only the increased volume of commercial work but also its largely unprecedented range; and there was regular recourse to the expedient of using English QCs as temporary Deemsters for particularly difficult cases, such as those of SIB and Steele v Paz. By 2008, the total number of practising advocates had risen to 171.

'The Top Division of Finance Centres'

The Isle of Man's image has not always been supported by official resources; but the long-serving Speaker of the House of Keys, Sir Charles Kerruish, later to become the Island's first President of Tynwald strove throughout his long political career to raise the Island's profile internationally, particularly within the Commonwealth. This was achieved not only by the staging of the Tynwald Millennium celebrations in 1979 and the Commonwealth Parliamentary Association meeting of 1984 in the Island, but through his personal efforts elsewhere. Occasionally Sir Charles allowed his enthusiasm to run away with him, as when he allowed himself to be mistaken as King Charles, King of the Isle of Man, in Dubai (a true story, picked up by *Private Eye* around 1989). Luckily, the witness to this event was able to allay disappointment by the discovery, in 1994, of another Isle of Man, located in the Nicobar Islands in the Bay of Bengal at 93E 9N; as the report says, it appears to be populated only by parrots and monkeys, but might make a convenient place for an alternative House of Keys, with a vacancy even for a king.[71]

All in all, over the two decades since 1985, the Island's business sector has enjoyed steady expansion, although it remains smaller than that of either of the larger Channel Islands, apart from in the field of life assurance. The standard of the work performed here has won numerous accolades from international surveys, all of which confirm the favourable conclusion of the Edwards report that the Island occupies a place in the 'top division of finance centres'. The impetus for this increase in business has come largely from within the resources of the firms themselves, although some measure of Governmental support has been forthcoming in the form of legislation, occasional road shows, the recent appointment of a marketing director of Isle of Man Finance, and the branding exercise 'Freedom to Flourish'.

CHAPTER 9

AS TIME GOES BY

The Changing Face of Tourism

During the 1960 debates on the abolition of Manx Surtax, emphasis was laid on the support of tourism and light manufacturing as alternatives to an influx of new residents. Throughout the 1960s and 1970s tourism continued to receive a measure of support, and new ventures were encouraged, such as modern self-catering accommodation in the Groudle Glen and Ballacarmel Holiday Cottages projects. The construction of the new Palace Hotel and the modernization and extension of the Castle Mona Hotel had taken place early on, and the Ramsey Hydro too had been refurbished at considerable expense and re-launched as the Grand Island Hotel. In addition, the Casino had been opened and the Summerland leisure complex built, (and rebuilt in 1978, after its destruction by fire in 1973).

However, many hoteliers and boarding-house keepers, conscious, even if they did not like to admit it, that the market had changed, were unwilling to incur the expense of bringing their establishments up to date for a short summer season and low rental rates. Many politicians however, persisted in maintaining, in the face of all the evidence to the contrary, that the old holiday trade was still capable of revival. During the period of the TT races, which was supported by considerable Government investment, (despite having received professional advice that it was a money loser for the Island) the Island was fully booked, and the Millennium celebrations of 1979 produced arrival figures as high as any in the past; but the downward trend was unmistakable.

Today, the Island's tourist industry focuses on special interest holidays, such as sporting fixtures (of which the TT races remain the most important), walking, fishing, and cultural tourism, the last of which has been encouraged by the consolidation of the Island's chief museums,

Hilberry Green, Douglas. A good example of one of the larger Mill Baldwin houses.

sites and monuments under the banner of Manx National Heritage. But the burgeoning finance sector has created its own demands for better accommodation, and this has been reflected in the refurbishment and extension of the Sefton and other Douglas hotels. But many of the Island's leading hotels were lost: the Fort Anne, Peveril, Villiers, and Douglas Bay gave way to offices, and many boarding-houses on Queen's Promenade were converted into flats. Tourist accommodation in Port St Mary, Peel and Ramsey, and Port Erin, apart from the new Cherry Orchard Hotel, is virtually a thing of the past. Although the remaining accommodation is of significantly higher quality, it is rarely fully booked.

Manufacturing

In manufacturing the picture has been similar; businesses have expanded or new ones have come, encouraged by Government support. But towards the end of the century, following a trend current throughout Western Europe and North America, companies began to close because they found themselves unable to compete with manufacturers in the Far East or even Eastern Europe. Among these were Ronaldsway Shoe Company and Eildon Fabrics, while Strix moved much of its production to China. The establishment in 1988 of a Freeport at Ronaldsway, with supporting legislation, was intended to attract suitable business; it provided tax relief on goods being brought in for warehousing or processing with a measure of confidentiality, an important consideration for the only major plant to be established, Pacini Ltd, a subsidiary of De Beers, involved in processing industrial artificial diamonds and manufacturing cutting tools at a time when South Africa was politically sensitive.

Unfortunately, one imaginative manufacturing venture did not succeed. In 1984 a team led by Major Malcolm Wren had been designing a new type of rigid airship, recalling the great pre-war designs of Zeppelin and others, which had come spectacularly to grief when they caught fire. Soft structures of airships (like barrage balloons with engines) had been produced but were limited in use. These rigid airships, using new less dangerous gases based on helium, promised a greater load-bearing capacity and the ability to stay aloft for long periods and land without runways in undeveloped parts of the world; they could also be used for military purposes, including surveillance. A new hangar for their construction was built at Jurby, and opened on 14th June 1988. In January 1989, however, the hangar was badly damaged by gales and the fabric of the first airship was ripped. By 1991, the project had run out of money, even though the first airship was ready for testing. The demolition of the Jurby hangar at the end of 1993 sounded the death-knell of an ambitious and potentially outstanding enterprise. The development of the Island's light industry, the third plank of the 1960 plans, had also become quiet. However, at the start of the new Millennium, several of the specialist design and engineering companies reinvented themselves; so that by 2008 there were sixteen aerospace companies operating, which supplied, for example, Boeing, Rolls Royce and the U.S. space programme. From 2004 the growth in manufacturing was around 30%, accounting for some 7% of GDP, and employing 2,500. The physical space of the Island facilitates the establishment of such manufacturing.

Property

Between 1979 and 1987 there was virtually no change in the population, and property prices remained weak. The advent of the Thatcher government in the UK may have been partly responsible. Exchange control was abolished, and the top rate of income tax progressively reduced from 98%, to 60% and finally to 40%. Capital Transfer Tax was changed into Inheritance Tax which was much the same but allowed for tax-free gifts during a donor's lifetime. The Isle of Man Government began to express the desirability of attracting 'economically active people', though at first this amounted to little more than the mouthing of a slogan.

But early in 1987 several local estate agents decided to stimulate the housing market by visiting Jersey and Guernsey, where they pointed out to residents that they could sell their houses in the Channel Islands and buy equivalent properties in the Isle of Man at half the cost. This strategy succeeded in attracting a number of new residents.[72] This influx of new residents coincided with the surge in financial business. There resulted an acute shortage of housing and prices shot up, provoking a further outbreak of protests, this time from a group calling themselves *FSFO*. Apart from a pause in demand and a fall in prices between 1989 and 1992, demand has remained steady and property prices have continued to rise, despite the large number of new houses that have been built, and despite the credit crises of 2007 which has affected property prices in the UK more strongly than in the Isle of Man.

Shipping and aircraft

However, neither the Government nor individuals have confined their aspirations to these established activities, including financial services. Quite properly they have cast around for other enterprises which might with advantage be based in the Island. Many of these display similar characteristics to those of financial services structures. In the early 1980s a series of Acts in the field of marine legislation (Safety of Life at Sea, &c.) had been introduced, up to modern standards, but providing a basis for the establishment of a Manx shipping register. The Manx register had

Douglas Head Apartments. This major apartment block picks up the feel and style of the former Douglas Head Hotel high above the harbour. It has preserved the 19th century marker tower.

existed as a British registry since 1786 but its use had been confined to ships having their main business in the Island, such as ferries, freighters and fishing boats. In 1984 a fully-serviced register was established for operating anywhere in the world; these vessels were registered in Douglas, flew the red ensign, and were surveyed to the highest standards. The new register enabled ship owners to establish companies in the Island free of tax, and to renegotiate union agreements with both seamen and officers on more realistic terms than those which had contributed to the decline of the British shipping industry, once the largest in the world. Crews working predominately overseas could avoid paying UK taxes, while preserving the benefits of their National Insurance contributions should they so desire. Ship management companies set up in the Island; many were seeking an alternative to Hong Kong whose future in the early 1980s was uncertain. The new register grew rapidly to surpass that of the UK,

Mooragh Promenade, Ramsey. The incomplete Victorian front has now been filled in with modern apartments.

by 2006 exceeding 9.123 million gross registered tonnage, including tanker fleets of Shell and BP. The registry is regarded as being of top quality; although it offers valuable tax advantages, in no way it is to be dismissed as a 'flag of convenience'. Recently there has been a move towards registering super-yachts, and by 2007 the register contained 403 ships, 49 commercial yachts and 350 pleasure yachts; in 2005/06 it was ranked the best ship register in the world in the International Flag State performance table.[73] On 1st May 2007 a similar register was set up for aircraft, opening with two locally owned aircraft using the prefix letter M; by the end of 2008 100 aircraft had been registered.

The Film Industry

Another new development which was has enjoyed some success has been the use of the Island as a location and base for films. Some thirty years earlier, 'Bergerac', a TV detective series, had been made based on

Jersey, with John Nettles in the title role as a police sergeant.[74]

The Manx Film Commission was set up in order to assist approve⌐ projects with tax exemption and, more importantly, finance, by investing up to 50% in a film, on condition that half of the budget was spent in the Isle of Man.[75] The Island was also widely used for locations, although it takes a keen eye to spot this. Two early films were set in Ireland, but filmed almost entirely in the Isle of Man, 'The Brylcream Boys', about prisoners of war, filmed in Jurby, and 'Waking Ned', about an Irishman who wins the lottery after his death. 'Waking Ned' was a great success; although it was shot in Cregneash, Niarbyl and other locations in the south and west of the Island, it attracted large numbers of tourists from the USA to visit Ireland. Lessons have been learned, and since then the base and film locations in the Island have been better labelled. The Island benefits financially, not only from the provision of accommodation, the restaurant trade, the employment of 'extras', and the use of the new film studios outside Ramsey, but, besides a share in any profits, from the fact that the VAT receipts fell outside the Common Purse section of the Customs and Excise Agreement. The alterations to the Common Purse definitions made in 2007 have removed much of the fiscal benefit of the film industry to the Island, and it remains to be seen if the 'industry' will continue; in any event, the studio near Ramsey which received financial and planning support from government had little use, little use was made of Manx individuals and virtually no support was given to the work of indigenous film makers.

E-commerce

The electronic revolution opened up a world of opportunity in E-commerce. Geographical remoteness in the new electronic age has become of little significance.

When telephone services were privatised in the UK, the Isle of Man Government took over responsibility within the Island from the UK, and, after a tendering process, awarded the service to Manx Telecom, a new subsidiary of British Telecom, subsequently split, and later taken over by the Spanish telephone service *Telefonica*. Manx Telecom used the Island as a test bed for new technical services such as broadband. New enterprises made possible by the new technology have included e-gaming, or gambling by means of e-mail. Punters anywhere in the world can be connected on line, foiling the best efforts of the US Government to outlaw on-line gaming on the grounds that it encourages money-laundering and thereby crime and terrorism. (Possibly the US authorities are merely anxious to protect their own gaming industry). Typical areas of gambling are poker games against other gamblers, and sports gambling which is particularly popular in Eastern Asia. In any event, gambling is a controversial subject, laying itself open to charges of involvement with criminal syndicates, and feeding addiction. It calls for powerful and efficacious legislation and supervision. Bearing in mind the moralistic attitudes that have been adopted towards the finance industry, and to the casino in earlier years, it is surprising that comparatively few objections to this activity have arisen in the Island, but this may be because the activities are virtually invisible within the Island. Nevertheless the amounts of money passing through the fifteen or so participant firms comes to several billions of dollars; and, being taxed on a sliding scale of turnover yields a handsome income to the Treasury, and employs several hundred people.

Ferry and Air Services

Communications with the rest of the world have always been crucial to the prosperity and accessibility of the Island. In the 1970s, at long last, ro-ro ferries were introduced when permission was granted for a linkspan to be placed in Douglas harbour, despite opposition from the Speaker, Charles Kerruish, who later criticized the Isle of Man Steam Packet for not having introduced this type of ship earlier. In 1978 a rival company, Manx Line, was set up with the *Manx Viking*, an elderly, basic ship sailing from Heysham; in 1985, this company amalgamated with the Steam Packet, discontinuing the main regular sea link with Liverpool. The combined company was owned by Jim Sherwood's Sea Containers and a new service agreement to use the two linkspans in Douglas harbour was put in place, imposing conditions on the company in terms of services and fares. The company was acquired in turn by the Macquarie Bank of

Queen's Mansions, Queen's Promenade, Douglas. The nearest block, designed in Regency style by Ellis Brown in 1989, did not sell well. The site was later completed with modern bays to the right.

Australia in 2006. In 1998 a new combined freight and passenger vessel, the *Ben-my-Chree*, was commissioned for the route between Douglas and Heysham (the nearest practical port to the Island); twice-daily sailings were scheduled throughout the year, and from 1994 less regular sailings using fast craft were reintroduced to Liverpool, and to Belfast and Dublin in the summer months. The Irish Sea does not lend itself to tranquil crossings on such craft, and the service is necessarily less reliable than that of conventional ships, despite the introduction, early in 2009, of a large catamaran, named *Manannan*.

Air services play a vital role in the Island's communications and now provide the usual link for business people. In 1960 British European Airways introduced De Havilland Rapides, shortly to be replaced with the relatively new Viscounts, which served the Island for some twenty years. Flights to Blackpool, Manchester, Liverpool and to Belfast were provided by Silver City and other airlines. British Airways (in its various guises such as Cambrian) periodically withdrew its services, as it was to do again in 2007. In 1982, the various carriers combined their services in Manx Airlines, a new service (although nominally it dated back to 1953); this was named as the national carrier and its aircraft bore the Manx Triskele on their tail fins. The force behind the new airline, both financially and technically, was British Midland, controlled by Sir Michael Bishop. In 1987 a British Aerospace 146, a four-engined jet, took over the flagship run to London's Heathrow from the viscounts. Under the management of Terry Lydiard the new airline flourished, floated, and expanded into providing low-volume routes between less important centres in the UK and the continent under a BA franchise, flying as BA City Express.

In 2001, just before the terrorist attacks on New York and Washington, British Airways offered a good price to take over British Regional Airways (the parent company of Manx Airlines) in order to secure these routes. However, the enterprise did not prosper in BA ownership, partly as a consequence of the post-9/11 difficulties experienced by the airline business. Re-launched as BA Connect the business was acquired by Flybe in March 2007. In the meantime the London service had been rerouted from Heathrow to the unpopular and inconvenient Gatwick, releasing to BA three valuable landing and take-off slots at Heathrow which they could use for other purposes.

A number of new airlines appeared to fill gaps or to compete with BA or Flybe, with an ever changing list of destinations. The largest of these, Euromanx, developed a useful route to London City, but also inexplicably competed directly with Flybe, most notably on the route to Manchester which already enjoyed ample provision. The resulting cut-price fares seemed to have brought the result of Euromanx's sudden collapse in March 2008. However, in January 2009 Aer Aran resumed the route to City Airport.

Reliable communications by air are essential for the Island. When BA ran the service it functioned well and international connections went smoothly. Manx Airlines, too, provided a good, reliable service as well as acting as an ambassador for the Island. The current range of available destinations and frequency of flights is impressive, but at the time of

Brewery Wharf, Castletown. Purpose built apartments of 1989 on the site of Castletown Brewery. The brewery offices on the right have been renovated.

writing there is a question mark over the reliability and financial viability of the operations.

Education

Offshore education was another idea that attracted a certain amount of interest. At secondary level the Island had regarded itself as a pioneer of comprehensive schools, a development to which the geography and population naturally lent itself, at any rate outside Douglas. After the Second World War new secondary schools were built in Castletown and Peel. The size and social mix of the schools were ideal for such unitary schools; the Island's Board of Education has, rather complacently, prided itself on this success, although in some respects they should expect more of their pupils to make the most of the opportunities of the modern world, especially those offered by the Island's flourishing professional and finance sectors. King William's College, the Island's only fee-paying public school for boys, effectively lost Government support for scholarships from the late 1980s; and absorbed its sister school, the Buchan School for Girls, which was experiencing financial difficulties. Under its recently retired Principal, Philip John, King William's has abandoned the increasingly unsatisfactory A level examinations in favour of the

The Malt House, Castletown. Another conversion in 1990 of the old warehouse of Castletown Brewery by the author with the help of Ellis Brown. It won an RIBA award.

International Baccalaureate. The school now attracts students from Germany and other parts of Europe and the Far East.

At tertiary level the Island's Board of Education had already expanded the provision for school leavers and mature students by combining professional craft courses, and the various colleges of art and domestic science, into a new College of Further Education which opened in 1973. The College also provided a base for degree courses, initially with the Open University. Despite the continued expansion of the College's role, by the 1980s there was ambitious talk of opening a University of Man. However, by 1999 the concept had been redefined as an International Business School where the emphasis would be on offshore operations. Despite the disadvantages of its layout and location, the historic Nunnery, situated in parkland on the outskirts of Douglas, was indirectly acquired by the Government. Its acquisition marks a further stage in the

Government's convoluted involvement with the Nunnery which it ha
purchased many years earlier for £50,000, but subsequently sold on t_
millionaire race-horse owner Robert Sangster. The most recent vendor,
Graham Ferguson Lacey, like Judah Binstock before him, demonstrated
his astuteness in a series of strategic acquisitions of properties which
were important Manx heritage sites, thereby placing the Government in a
dilemma.[76]

Another educational enterprise was the International Hotel School,
originally based in a hotel in Port Erin; this offered training in all aspects
of the hospitality industry, as well as English language skills to students
who came principally from the Far East. After many years the School
closed abruptly in April 2007 leaving the last students stranded, penniless
and without the qualifications that they had expected, thus presenting
another problem for the Manx Government.

Employment Legislation

During this period, quite apart from nationalist agitation, there was
considerable union unrest led by the Transport and General Workers'
Union local secretaries, John Corrin (TGWU 1979-86) and his successor,
Bernard Moffatt. When John Corrin retired in 1986 upon election to the
House of Keys, he moved sharply to the right, resolutely opposing the
abolition of birching and hanging and the reforms embodied in the
Sexual Offences and Human Rights legislation. Both Corrin and Moffatt
played a major role in a series of disputes involving shipping, fuel
workers, the brewery, printers, journalists, gas workers, electricians,
plumbers and finally, in July 1987, a one-day general strike. In most
respects, the Island's employment legislation lagged behind that of the
UK, particularly the Thatcher reforms on strike ballots and secondary
picketing; also, the unions, not wholly unreasonably, sought to share in
some of the prosperity engendered by the Island's new activities in the
form of better pay, equal pay, redundancy provision, and a minimum
wage. The Emergency Powers Act of 1988 and the Trade Union and
Employment Act of 1991 gave the Government a certain amount of
control. Industrial relations, perhaps in consequence, have greatly

improved since the 1990s and the fiery rhetoric has been replaced by sensible solutions though the Union had only limited success in enlisting the sympathies of the staff of banks and financial service companies.[77]

Disquiet and agitation about new developments within the Island was not confined to unions and their leaders. Many ordinary Manx people were puzzled and distressed by what they rightly saw as a fundamental change to the Island, as big as any in their history alongside the arrival of the Vikings, the English under the Stanleys and the advent of mass tourism. This disquiet found particularly colourful expression in the 1970s and 80s.

CHAPTER 10

'O LAND OF OUR BIRTH!'

Reaction

When any community confronts new and potentially threatening changes some reaction is to be expected. It was not only economic development that provoked a fierce reaction from the locals, but also the supercilious demeanour of some newcomers. The Isle of Man had experienced a large influx of people, largely of English origin, some of whom came to the Island by way of the colonies or Ireland; many incomers displayed neither understanding of the Island nor sympathy for its people and their way of life. Although many arrivals fitted in well, others remained aloof in their own exclusive communities; their behaviour was often perceived as insensitive and arrogant. Condescending references to the 'natives' on the part of newcomers who behaved as if they were still expatriates living in a colony scarcely contributed to a climate of mutual tolerance and respect. Some Anglo-Irish and English newcomers (not, on the whole, the ex-colonial civil servants) threw their weight about, unaware that the Manx are a small nation with a long and proud history, and a classless tradition devoid of any notions of deference.

Furthermore, by the early seventies economic pressure was intensifying; this was most apparent in the soaring land and property prices. In 1960 the property market had been in severe decline with lack of demand depressing property values below their usual modest level. Any increase in population was bound to lead to a sudden rise in prices, even without the influx of rich and even the not-so-rich people from outside the Island. One of the grievances which exercised the minds of local people was the fact that ordinary Manx people who were not in the top wage bracket were unable to raise sufficient capital for a deposit which would have enabled them to get a foot on the property ladder. The

Charred remains of a £20,000 bungalow at Ballasalla with another, half completed, in the background, 1973.

cost of rented accommodation, too, rose steadily, despite the fact that part of the demand for more housing was satisfied by the surge in house-building, assisted by relaxed official attitudes towards planning.

The tension between supply and demand in the housing market is virtually inevitable in a market economy (as opposed to a command economy like that of Soviet Russia). Most market economies, including those of the UK, Ireland and the Isle of Man continue to be affected by this phenomenon. Quite apart from the effects of general inflation and the increased pressure on services (hospitals, schools, roads, utilities), the only solution to rising demand is to increase the area of land released for building. This in turn raises environmental issues and anxiety about the despoliation of the countryside. All these factors provoked storms of protest in some quarters in the Island.

These protests against development took little account of the other side of the coin: without the growth in population figures and the expansion of business, the Isle of Man would have entered a period of decline, making it impossible to maintain even a modest level of infrastructure. New resources were essential, not only to pay for developments but to maintain and modernize existing facilities. Regardless of persistent claims to the contrary and despite the best efforts, the Island's traditional activities of farming, fishing, tourism, and even the new manufacturing industry, would have been incapable of generating the resources that were needed; this is, of course, not to say that efforts in these areas should not have been vigorously pursued.

Protest Movements: the 1960s and 70s

The keenest protests were directed against individuals perceived to be profiteering, especially members of Tynwald who were believed to be taking advantage of their position. A strong moral stance was assumed by the protesters, not only against profiteering, but against the whole concept of the Island's status as a tax haven. Protesters objected both to individuals who had taken up residence to escape the increasingly severe taxation of the UK, and the new financial institutions and structures based in the Island.

First to organize systematic opposition to the new policies was *Mec Vannin* (Sons of Man) formed in 1963. The party fielded a wide selection of candidates in the 1971 Keys elections.[78] However, their efforts were largely unsuccessful as the electorate still tended to support the traditional, better-known candidates; in consequence, the *Fo Halloo* (Underground) movement emerged. This commanded widespread sympathy and support amongst a significant number of Island people of all ages and persuasions, motivated by a sense of despair born of the conviction that the protests of ordinary citizens went unheard, while those with money, land and power were despoiling the Island for their own profit. Their activities manifested themselves in protests, a newssheet, direct action and finally arson. The protesters gained considerable attention, not only within the Isle of Man but also in the UK media, on Granada News, in TV interviews and in newspapers such as the *Daily Mail*. The movement received scant support either from those in Government or from the Manx newspapers controlled by H. L. Dor and John Christian, but for a while they had strong support from the *Manx Star*, edited by Valerie Cottle.

Much of the protest was conveyed in the pages of the *Fo Halloo Free Manx Press*, of which twenty issues were circulated between March 1973 and November 1976. Although it was claimed that the editor took great pains to ensure the accuracy of the contents, it has to be understood that there was not necessarily any independent evidence for many of the allegations or comments. However, nobody claimed authorship, and no one was available to be pursued for defamation since the publication was entirely anonymous, which was in itself illegal.

The issues enjoyed mocking several of the targets, not only those who, like Judah Binstock, were clearly active in property speculation, but also prominent Manx politicians who had supported the abolition of Manx surtax, or who had themselves bought or sold property during the period, and leading Athol Street professionals.

The newssheet, of which only the last two issues were properly printed, was typed and cyclostyled surrepticiously on government equipment and widely distributed by volunteers. The cost of preparing the newssheet was raised by donations from sympathisers; it was welcomed by readers who relished the *skeet*, or gossip, about prominent figures and the (often scurrilous) cartoons and verses.

The extracts which have been included are designed to give a flavour of the comments of the time and should not necessarily be regarded as true; but they had wide circulation and were greatly enjoyed by the Manx public, even if some also deplored some of the more scurrilous allegations and mockery of the Island and its leading figures.

Some of the protests came from the main players of *Fo Halloo*, but there were other, more extreme actions by people on the fringe of the movement. These peripheral activities contributed to the ultimate decline of the movement, along with the difficulty of sustaining a loose, voluntary, unfunded protest movement for a prolonged period, in this case more than four years. During *Fo Halloo*'s brief lifetime there were some spectacular and effective protests, including the daubing of slogans, and the widespread use of posters, distributed by people of all ages. Slogans were burnt onto headlands, and a fiery cross set alight near Tynwald Hill in 1973. In July 1974 protesters climbed on to Tynwald Hill itself during the annual ceremony before the arrival of the official procession and brandished placards proclaiming 'Stop the Sell-out', 'Close this Tax Haven', 'The Island for Sale' and 'Tynwald Equals Government and Self-Interest'.[79]

On another occasion all the locks of professional and banking offices in Athol Street were filled up with superglue overnight by a group of supporters comprising, for the most part, pensioners. Builders' marking pegs were removed from development sites and in March 1973, a bungalow in Ballasalla under construction by an associate of Judah Binstock, the property speculator, was set on fire.

Fo Halloo - **Free Manx Press**

The *Fo Halloo* newssheets identify the movement's particular targets. Among politicians, J. B. Bolton and Percy Radcliffe attracted special opprobrium, John Bolton for his association with Judah Binstock, and Percy Radcliffe for selling off large areas of his farmland to developers (always referred to as 'speculators'). The land deals of the Speaker, Charles Kerruish, attracted regular mention, as did Athol Street professionals. Here are some examples from Issue No. 2 of April 1973, which refer to some of the specific complaints:

[Although not an actual page, we have given a selection of the comments to give a flavour of what was being said]:

CHRISTIAN (J J) AWAKE - YOU'RE SEEN AS JUDAH'S TOOL
- The Manx Hansard's not worth it.

EXODUS
When Judah on a trip one day
Came to the Isle of Man,
He said, "I'd like to buy the place,"
J Bolton said, "You can.
We'll set a price that's not too high
To start a lot of noise,
The one and only stipulation being
Jobs for all the Boys."

Cartoons in Fo Halloo Free Manx Press.

"You can make the regulations,
And we will all obey,
For we haven't the moral courage
To manage any other way."
Said Judah, waving cheques for all the banks.
Said Bolton, "We'll keep the speculators
And throw out all the Manx."

****

For Sale: Percy Radcliffe - offers

****

ARSON
Poor Judah's very cross indeed,
His house burned to the ground.
Good luck, whoever did the deed,
We hope you're never found.

Oh, what a shameful, wicked blow
To one who loves us well,
But if we saw the fuses glow,
There's not a soul would tell.

We all should bow our heads in shame
And tremble at the threat,
Dear Judah's friends will quit this game,
If we too uppish get.

He hasn't sense to see what's plain,
To love him we're not able,
Except those few who grab the grain,
He spills beneath the table.

They are the rogues, the knaves, the cheats,
Our own Manx kith and kin.
Some day we'll trust they'll feel the heat,
And pay for all their sin.

The fiery cross has burned before,
The natives rose and fought,
Pay heed and give no cause for more,
Lest gains be dearly bought.

In the next edition, No. 3, the following extracts from the *Daily Telegraph* were reprinted which show severe criticisms of many of the most influential of the members of Tynwald of the time. This edition drew attention to many land deals involving not only Judah Binstock, but many leading members of the Manx establishment, not least members of Tynwald itself. They are here set out in some detail to show the extent and force of the criticism, and as an expression of the powerlessness of ordinary Manx people:

Following an independent investigation into the property dealings of members of the Manx Government by a senior reporter, a series of articles appeared in the 'Daily Telegraph' recently. For those who have not seen them, this news-sheet contains extracts from the articles, which illustrate the decadent arrogance of those whom you elected to serve the best interests of the community and whose decisions hold sway over the futures of sixty thousand people and control the destiny of the Manx nation.

Claims by Isle of Man nationalists that some members of Tynwald, the Island's Parliament, have been involved in land deals or business associations with property developers are supported by documents in the Manx general registry of deeds and companies.

Documents show that Mr Henry Charles Kerruish, Speaker of the House of Keys, has sold land to a Paris-based developer, Mr Judah Binstock, and Mr John James Bell, Chairman of Tynwald's Airports Board, has been a director of one of Mr Binstock's companies.

A deed filed in the Manx High Court general registry in Douglas shows that in March last year Mr Kerruish sold an unspecified number of acres in Lonan parish for £25,000 to Mr Binstock's company, Isle of Man and Overseas Estates Corp., which recently increased its nominal share capital from £1 million to £2 million.

The file of Bunting Construction Co., a £2,000 nominal capital subsidiary of Isle of Man and Overseas Estates Corp. shows that Mr Bell was a director with Mr Binstock in 1971-72 and was still a director in the latest return dated Feb. 27th this year.

When interviewed at the Palace Hotel about the attacks that have been made upon him, Mr Binstock joked: 'I'm the bogey-man and the big bad wolf because I am buying land like crazy. They are a tight little community and they get worried when they see people like myself coming in from outside and buying land. You're a foreigner here unless you have lived on the Island for 300 years'.

He declined to say how much land he had bought. 'Enough', he said with a laugh. Why was he buying it? 'Because of tax reasons and the falling value of the pound. Land in the Isle of Man is a good investment'.

Mr Binstock, once a well known personality in the London casino and property world, and author of a book on casino gambling said he now lived in Paris but was domiciled in another country.

When asked to comment on the propriety of their connections with Mr Binstock, Mr Kerruish was 'not available', Mr Bell said before going out for the evening from his home in St Ninian's Road, Douglas, 'I don't make comments over the phone'.

MANX SPEAKER IN £50,000 LAND DEALS

Mr Henry Charles Kerruish, Speaker of the House of Keys in the Isle of Man, has made more than £50,000 worth of land and property purchases in the Island in the past 20 months, inquiries at the Manx Land Registry have disclosed.

His property purchases included a house in Ramsey, which he bought for £3,750 in February last year and is now offering it for sale through estate agents for £12,000. The price being asked for is an example of soaring property value on the Island following big land purchases by outside developers.

The property in Ramsey is one of four purchases which he made in January, February, April and June last year which totalled £51,250.

"WE TYNWALD MEMBERS HAVE ALWAYS BELIEVED IN HOME OWNERSHIP —— I PERSONALLY OWN OVER A HUNDRED & FIFTY."

Cartoon in Fo Halloo Free Manx Press.

MANX LEADER SILENT ON LAND DEALS

Mr Percy Radcliffe, chairman of the Executive Council of the Isle of Man Government, and one of the architects of its drive to attract new-residents to the Island, has sold two properties for more than £28,000 to English buyers in the past 12 months.

Conveyances showed that Mr Radcliffe, described in the documents as a member of the House of Keys, sold a house and land for £22,000 to a woman in Cheshire last December and a cottage and land to a man in Manchester for £6,750 last August.

The £28,000 sales by Mr Radcliffe to two English buyers were among sales of land and buildings totalling more than £45,000 made by him in the two parishes of Lezayre and Ballaugh, in the Northern part of the Island, in the past four years.

As chairman of the Executive Council, Mr Radcliffe, 56, a farmer, is the Island's 'Prime Minister'.

Mr Radcliffe is also chairman of the Island's Local Government Board, the planning authority which authorised waiving of building bye-laws so that the £2 million Summerland Centre in Douglas, which burnt down with 49 deaths this month, could be built.

As well as the reports in the *Daily Telegraph*, and the assertions in the *Fo Halloo* newssheet, there were protests on these property deals by MHKs from within Tynwald itself as the *Telegraph* also reported:

MANX MP'S DEALING IN TAKEOVER OF LAND ATTACKED
Members of the Isle of Man Parliament who have been involved in land deals or business associations with property developers were attacked last night by Mr Roy MacDonald, a member of the House of Keys.
'I don't think members should dabble in this sort of thing. It's a question of moral standards'.
Mr MacDonald, who has been pressing for a compulsory register of Tynwald members interests, said: 'You expect parliamentarians to set the highest standards.
I don't mind members who have land selling it to people who are going to work the land or live on it. What I object to is people who buy land to resell it at a profit'.
Mr MacDonald said he did not think Mr Kerruish would face questions about his land deals when the House reassembled. 'There are too many other members in the same boat,' he said.

****

ARE YOU PREPARED TO LEAVE YOUR FUTURE IN THE HANDS OF THESE PEOPLE? PEOPLE WHO PLACE THEIR BUSINESS INTERESTS BEFORE THE WELFARE OF THE ISLAND? IT IS THREE YEARS UNTIL THE NEXT ELECTION AND BY THEN IT WILL BE TOO LATE. THEIR RESIGNATIONS MUST BE DEMANDED NOW AND THEY BE REMOVED FROM THE HIGH OFFICES THEY HAVE DEGRADED. THE ANSWER IS IN YOUR HANDS: IT IS YOUR FUTURE AND THAT OF YOUR CHILDREN THAT IS AT STAKE!

It has to be said in defence of the people mentioned that such sales were not necessarily in any way improper in themselves, nor more than taking advantage of the changes in land use within the Island. But to the ordinary Manxman the perception of profiteering was distasteful.

The next comment in edition 5 was more pertinent and drew attention to what appeared to be an MHK taking improper advantage of his position, in the case of John J. Bell, who, as chairman of the Airport Board had obtained the contract for painting the airport for his own firm:

> Not content with tapping and taping telephone conversations, our hero from the 'Waterpaint Affair', J. J. Bell, MHK, now moves to underhand tricks to show up the Airport Security Staff. How can constituents have any confidence in such people to look after their interests in Government?

But Roy MacDonald, MHK for Peel was not the only MHK to notice his colleagues' dealings. In Issue 10 of 1974 the quote of the month features the response of Percy Radcliffe, MHK, chairman of the local Government Board and Planning Committee, himself criticised for land sales in issue 3, in reply to an attack by Speaker Charles Kerruish. Mr Radcliffe used some pertinent research to make his point:

> I have here a list, which I have been previously reluctant to use, of planning applications made by the honourable Mr Speaker between October 1965 and November 1972, a period of seven years. It contains 33 applications for more than 72 dwellings of one type or another, on land in his possession in the parishes of Maughold, Lonan and German. In fact some of the applications are for more than one dwelling, and one is for no less than 23 building plots. Never in the history of Tynwald has one Member speculated in so much land for such self-interest over such a short period of time.

This statement in Tynwald could hardly be more damning, yet even this did not dampen the Speaker's appetite for land deals, as his involvement in the Ballacarmel Holiday Cottages affair was to show some ten years later. This issue became the subject of a Tynwald enquiry.

The general theme of the protests is encapsulated by a satirical version of the Lord's Prayer:

WHAT TO LOOK FOR IN A GREAT M.H.K

HEAD LOOK FOR THICKNESS, THIS MAKES OUTSTANDING M.H.Ks. TWO FACED M.H.Ks HAVE AN OBVIOUS ADVANTAGE

EARS. SHOULD ALWAYS BE DEAF TO PUBLIC OPINION AND CRITICISM

HEART. THIS WILL HAVE BEEN REPLACED BY A BULGING WALLET

HANDS. GREAT M.H.Ks ALWAYS HAVE THESE CUPPED READY TO ACCEPT BACKHANDERS

TROUSERS. THESE WILL ALWAYS BE WORN AT THE KNEES DUE TO EXCESSIVE CRAWLING

FEET. BEST M H KS TRY TO KEEP AS FEW ON THE GROUND AS POSSIBLE.

Cartoon in Fo Halloo Free Manx Press.

Our Father, which art in Athol Street
Bolton be thy name
Should thy Kingdom come
We will be done on earth and probably
In heaven. Give us this day our
Dearer bread, and forgive us our
Trespassing on Mimi's [80] plot as we
Forgive them that speculate against us.
Lead us not into English ways
But deliver us from the common purse
For this is our Island.... No power
No glory, for ever and ever, AMEN

and also by a version of the Manx National Anthem:

A REVISED MANX NATIONAL ANTHEM?
O Isle of great worth
They're despoiling your earth,
For whatever the market will bear,
Build like a fool,
To hell with home rule,
All that's left is the free mountain air.

When Manxmen refrain,
From speculative gain,
Then will Ellan Vannin be free,
Ye sons of the soil
They don't value your toil,
And give Europe the fruits of our sea.

So we have a choice,
Give protest a voice,
And make Tynwald pay heed to our plea,
But what if we fail?
Leave our homeland on sale,
Our Isle would best sink in the sea.

The *Fo Halloo* newssheets also contain more substantial statements of opinion or policy which present the various issues more seriously. Issue 4 of June 1973 sums up the group's attitude towards speculators and 'tax dodgers':

> As Tynwald Day approaches, Manxmen would do well to consider whether this ceremony any longer has any significance, when our claims to independence and national integrity have been reduced to mere pretence. Debased by successive governments, it remains today as little more than a commercialised tourist attraction, with Tynwald's puppets acting out the characters. A day of national bondage, when Manxmen meet, not to celebrate their independence, but to pay homage to the British Crown and the almighty pound!
>
> The government's policy of selling the Island to the highest bidder has given financial control of Mann to a small band of capitalist manipulators, who invariably place profit before people. Our only natural resource, the land, is also rapidly falling under complete non-Manx control. Manxmen have been stripped of their pride and self-respect and forced to join the rat-race, chasing the proverbial 'quick-buck' as an only means of survival.
>
> The Isle of Man has become a pawn in the game of international finance, with the full backing of the Manx government! If this is allowed to continue, and if the number of immigrant tax-dodgers continues to spiral, then we can foresee only one eventuality.... Full integration with the United Kingdom!
>
> This would mean nothing to our present financial masters, as they will only move on to fresh pastures. But for the Isle of Man and genuine Manx people, such a move can only spell disaster.
>
> Fo Halloo believes that the time has come for Manxmen to fight back or forever hold their peace!
>
> We must fight the speculators; we must fight the developers; we must fight the manipulators; most of all we must fight the government. We must grasp every opportunity, however small, to prevent the ultimate takeover!
>
> THE MANX CROSS IS BURNING! GET OFF YOUR KNEES NOW.... GIVE TYNWALD DAY SOME MEANING. THE ANSWER LIES IN YOUR HANDS... STOP THE SELL-OUT TODAY!

As time went on, the political philosophy of the writer(s) hardened beyond attacks on individuals and speculators, beyond simple independence for the Island, to a rejection of capitalist and market forces in a form of socialism by common ownership of the land and national resources (whatever they may have been); this is expressed in issue 15 of 1975.

> In the coming months, the certainty of a constitutional clash between the Manx and United Kingdom governments over the implications of the Labour Government's proposed Finance Act now seems inevitable. As a result, talk of, and support for complete independence for the Island will undoubtedly increase. It is a cause we have long supported, both from an economic point of view and also as the unassailable right of any nation, regardless of size, to self-determination.
>
> But when you talk of Manx Freedom, do you mean only the freedom of the chemical elements which compose the soil of Mann? Or is it the Manx people you mean? If the latter, from what do you propose to free them? From the rule of the United Kingdom?
>
> If you were to remove the British presence tomorrow and hoist the Manx flag over Government House, unless you set about the organisation of a more equitable and just society, based on a common ownership of our national wealth, your efforts would be in vain.
>
> Britain would still rule you. She would rule you through her capitalists through her landlords, through her financiers, through the whole array of commercial institutions she has planted in this country, all of which have been encouraged and fostered by the quislings who control our own 'government' and who have been lining their own pockets and those of their friends and families, while ignoring the primary needs of the Manx economy and the Manx people!
>
> Britain would still rule you to your ruin, even while your lips offered hypocritical homage at the shrine of that Freedom whose cause you had betrayed!
>
> As Manxmen we are prepared to do all we can to achieve for our country her rightful heritage...... independence; what we are not prepared to support is an independence designed to maintain the

privileges and rule of those who have prostituted our island, destroyed its heritage and abused their positions to exploit for their personal gain, the labour and needs of ordinary Manxmen!

Remember, true patriotism seeks the welfare of each in the happiness of all, and is inconsistent with the selfish desire for profit which can only be gained by the exploitation of those less favoured in our community.

To you, people of Mann, we address ourselves, AGITATE in the workshop, in the field, in the factory, in the office, until you arouse your friends to oppose the system of which we are all the victims. EDUCATE, that the people may no longer be deluded by the illusory heroes of prosperity under any system that is controlled by bankers, accountants, landlords and tax-dodgers. ORGANISE, form your own groups to fight and purge the Manx Establishment of those whose narrow-minded greed has brought us all to the brink of disaster!

Only when power is in the hands of all of the people, and the exploitation of our Island from within has ceased can we talk of a meaningful independence. Always remember that the powerful only appear so to us because we are on our knees.

These opinions are strong meat, both nationalist and socialist, and revolutionary in their intentions, although containing strong elements of nostalgia.

The argument is developed to its final position in *Fo Halloo* 17, with the advocacy of a 'Socialist Republic of Mann'. This position was, and to a degree continues to be, espoused by some members of *Mec Vannin*. But by this time the simple philosophy of disquiet at what was happening and mockery of some of the people involved turned into a comprehensive, revolutionary political philosophy which attracted little popular support.

THE NEW RESIDENTS POLICY

The decision by Tynwald to attract large numbers of New Residents to the Island is, obviously, one of the most important and controversial it has ever made. This article will try to show, as dispassionately as possible, why this policy can only mean disaster for Ellan Vannin.

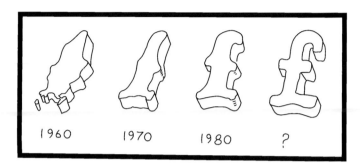

Cartoon in Fo Halloo Free Manx Press.

Unfortunately, in the tradition of a highly materialist society and in the aftermath of the "you've never had it so good" philosophy of the 1950s the human now spends a disproportionate amount of its time pursuing the acquisition of material wealth. It is this desire for material wealth (or "a higher standard of living" as it is politely called) which has prompted the introduction of the new residents policy.

"Poverty is a temporary fault; excessive wealth is a lasting ailment:" Kahziz Gibran.

Ten or twenty years ago the "traditional" forms of economic activity in Mannin: tourism, agriculture and fishing, were sufficient to fulfil basic need and to provide a small surplus for some individuals to indulge in the tempting (but, arguably, essentially worthless) offerings of consumerism. These traditional forms of economic activity have been recklessly abandoned in favour of the new residents policy and "high" finance.

FOR A SOCIALIST REPUBLIC OF MANN

In order for Mannin to survive as an independent nation we must re-think our whole industrial and agricultural policy. Although, as nationalists have pointed out for years, independence does not mean isolation, it does mean we must produce the things we need to live on in our own country, and considering the fact that we have always been basically an agricultural community surrounded by the sea, the importation of fruit, vegetables, milk products, eggs, and even fish, illustrates for all to see the disastrous inefficiency of our legislators. We therefore recommend that the following steps be implemented.

1. The nationalisation of all development land, all essential services and any natural resources which lie within our national boundaries.
2. The severance of all links between members of government, judiciary etc, with developers and speculative land/finance companies.
3. A method be devised which would ensure that those in Tynwald who have benefited from their recent speculative gains would be prevented from taking part in any future political activity.
4. The removal of all crown representatives and agents from the legislature.
5. Encouragement to be given to the fostering of our native language and culture.
6. The establishment of a closer economic and cultural bond between ourselves and the other Celtic nations.

Whether such a policy would ever be acceptable to the people of the Island, even to those born here, and whether Socialism anywhere in the world has proved to be the answer to popular needs is dubious; perhaps this explains why support for this brand of nationalism has not succeeded except in times of greatest provocation. In the meantime, in April 1973, the acknowledged nationalist party, *Mec Vannin* petitioned the Queen to prorogue Tynwald and institute a full inquiry into corruption.

Towards the end the *Fo Halloo* movement was running out of active support and funds, and by the end of 1976 overt activity had effectively ceased, even though many of the Island's inhabitants continued to be distressed by the developments they witnessed. In some cases dissatisfaction found expression not only in the extreme form of arson but in a generally hostile attitude towards newcomers, as evidenced by a circular issued in October 1973, ostensibly by *Fo Halloo*, but disavowed by most supporters.

FOR THE ATTENTION OF ALL NEW RESIDENTS:
As a new resident on OUR island, you are probably under the impression that you have been accepted by the Manx people. This is

Cartoon in Fo Halloo Free Manx Press.

far from the truth and we feel that it is necessary to make you aware that your very existence here is imposing a way of life totally alien to Manx tradition.

Manxmen are being forced into poor quality houses and flats, while your ever increasing numbers are placing an intolerable strain on our social services, schools, roads etc. Our island is being destroyed to cater for you and the tax-dodging activities that have been attracted here with you.

You would be well advised to heed our warning as all your future activities will undergo close scrutiny and appropriate reprisals will be taken against you for:-

a) Any acts considered to be contrary to the wishes or well-being of the Manx people, whether physical, social or financial.

b) Any dealings in property, land or other natural resources which may be interpreted as being in any way speculative.

Remember, you are only a resident alien in our country and as such
you must consider yourself a probable target in the continuing fight
to save our Island.

SEOSE LESH YN ASHOON VANNINAGH!

Issued for and on behalf of the Manx people by Fo Halloo.

The New Wave of Protests: the 1980s

Towards 1979 the first wave of development had died down and land
speculation had ceased to be profitable (as Richard Brooks, already
referred to, was to learn, to his cost). However, the anxiety about dubious
financial deals proved to have been only too well founded as
demonstrated when a number of private banks collapsed, most notably
the Savings and Investment Bank in 1982. Notwithstanding, by 1987 a
renewed influx of people and business was reviving the Island's property
market, a buoyant situation which has continued, with a pause in 1990 and
1991 to the present day. The initial resentment which had inspired *Fo
Halloo* had lain dormant rather than evaporated; it was rekindled by the
various banking collapses of the 1980s. The upsurge of development
sparked the spectacular re-emergence of this unrest.

The authors of its new manifestation were a small but influential
group led by Chris Sheard, a garden designer, Gregory Joughin, a
musician and dry-stone-waller, and Philip Gawne, a biochemistry
graduate who had been articled to the accountancy firm of Peat Marwick
and had worked on the liquidation of the SIB. Disenchanted by this last
experience Gawne had left Peat Marwick and dissociated himself from
everything the finance sector stood for. The protests of this group
stemmed from the sense that the business community and its members
were alien to the traditions of the Island, and that traditional activities like
agriculture, fishing and tourism were being neglected, as was the Island's
rich cultural heritage.

In essence the new protest was recognized as a resurgence of the
protests of the 1970s. However, now the protest did not take the form of
newssheets which enjoyed widespread support, but of direct action. The
first incident in 1988 arose almost spontaneously; after Chris Sheard's

Mystery slogan on railway bridge near St John's, 1988.

22nd birthday party the three friends went up to the road near South Barrule and repainted the slogan 'Tax dodgers go home' on the spot where it had originally been painted by *Fo Halloo*. (Unfortunately, as they had painted behind their car, the trio had to return to Peel the long way round to avoid the freshly applied paint). Having the necessary professional gardening equipment to hand, they next targeted the 'For Sale' signs of Cowley Groves, estate agents, chopping them down and planting one of them on the summit of Tynwald Hill. They daubed their new acronym, '*FSFO*', widely, often using sites previously used by *Fo Halloo* a dozen years earlier. On Tynwald Day they burnt with weed killer the initials '*FSFO*' in giant letters on Beary Mountain where it could be seen by all attending the ceremony. Their aims included the desire to destabilize the Government and halt the growth of financial services and new residents, and to attract attention to their concerns not only internally, but also in the consciousness of the UK and the outside world. In this they had a fair measure of success, but the movement lasted only nine months. In November 1988 the three ringleaders were arrested after

FSFO protestor being removed from Tynwald Hill, 1988.

setting fire to two houses under construction in Johnny Watterson's Lane, Douglas.[81] One of the three was so enthused by the quick burning of the first house that he prevailed on them to continue with a second. Unfortunately the delay allowed them to be observed by a neighbour who was able to identify their car which was distinct, if not unique, in the

Arson off Johnny Watterson's Lane, November 1988.

Island both in model and colour. They were subsequently convicted of arson and served prison terms but there was a popular feeling that Henry Callow, the Second Deemster, had been lenient in his sentencing out of a latent sympathy for their sentiments.

The acronym *FSFO* occasioned a good deal of speculation. Probably the majority believed that the first two letters stood for Finance Sector, and the last two accordingly. Many alternative interpretations were offered, including 'Fat Seagulls Fall Over', 'Folk Society Fund Organizer', 'Frigmund Seud Freaks Out', and 'Flowers Subdue Ferret Odour', but it is held that the letters stood for '*Fo Sostyn Fo Ordaag*', Manx for 'Under England, under the thumb'. FSFO badges were sported on Tynwald Day, even by some serving members of the House of Keys, including Mrs Hazel Hannan, MHK for Peel, and, with somewhat dark humour, souvenir match wallets were produced with FSFO emblazoned on the front.

Greg Joughin, Chris Sheard and Phil Gawne being led away after sentencing.

New Awareness

Though neither series of protests had any material effect on the Island's development in respect of either financial services or new residents, the protesters achieved their chief objective, that of making the Island's Government and its inhabitants, whether Manx or 'come-overs', aware of some important issues. Pressure on land and housing has continued unabated, apart from a brief lull between 1989 and 1992, and extensive investment has been needed for utilities, health and education; considerable expenditure would have been required even without the growth in population, as much of the Island's infrastructure was over a hundred years old and due for replacement.

But the nationalist movements also promoted a sense of Man's history and its identity as a distinct, if small, nation in the British Isles, alongside England, Wales, Scotland, and especially Ireland, whose Celtic origins and culture, and the strong Viking influence, bore considerable similarities to the Island's own. Groups of people, both Manx-born and 'come-overs' met regularly for cultural and political activities. From such beginnings there arose a revival of interest in Manx language, music and dancing, expressed informally in pubs and meetings, particularly *Eisteddfods* and *Yn Chruinnaght*, the Inter-Celtic cultural festival of music, dance and literature held every summer, originally in Ramsey.

Additionally, the establishment of the Manx Heritage Foundation, which supports Manx cultural endeavours of many kinds, and the Centre for Manx Studies, an academic centre under the University of Liverpool, have promoted research into many Manx-related subjects. Previous publications had largely been the work of gifted amateurs and antiquaries, or studies by individuals from outside the Island. Miles Walker, as Chief Minister, invited comments from the public, and, as a consequence of the volume of responses, set up a 'Quality of Life' Mori Poll which showed, inter alia, strong interest in all things Manx, including Manx Gaelic. 36% of parents were interested in the provision of Manx Gaelic on the school curriculum and an even higher proportion actually took up the option when it was offered. In 2001, partly in response to the requirement for more regional emphasis within the UK's national curriculum, and partly through local interest, the teaching of Manx history and culture became part of the school curriculum; this included the establishment of a Manx-medium school at primary level in St John's.

Despite the fall in proportion of Manx-born inhabitants compared to those born elsewhere (from 67.2% in 1961 to 47.55% in 2006, although the actual numbers of Manx-born[82] rose during the same period from 32,345 to 38,069 but were absorbed in the increasing population), the revival of interest in Manx culture has been largely successful, even among many who, although not of Manx origin, have committed their lives to the Island. This point of view is now strongly represented in Tynwald; Philip Gawne, one of the arsonists, is now MHK for Rushen and has been appointed Minister for the traditional area of Agriculture, Fisheries and Forestry. His ability to voice concerns relating to cultural or environmental issues at the highest level of decision-making, within the Council of Ministers, is invaluable. In contrast, the leadership of *Mec*

spokesman said he was delighted with the smooth manner in which the day had proceeded. He conceded that numbers planes, military helicopters and large numbers of Army and police officers swarmed through the village on Sunday and Monday.

F.S.F.O. badge boom!

UNDOUBTEDLY one of the most popular items on sale at the Tynwald Day Fair at St. John's were the F.S.F.O. badges.

While sale of the badges provided great amusement for both sellers and purchasers it certainly seemed to attract more than just a passing interest from the security men present on the fairground.

Heavy men with heavy cameras kept appearing from behind stalls and barriers to take photographs of those selling and wearing the badges, in particular the people doing displays of Manx traditional dancing.

One of the dancers said, "It was quite ridiculous the way these men kept popping up — maybe they should have read the badges first."

The badges each contained four words, the first letters of each word in bright colours and forming F.S.F.O. There were many different slogans on the badges and we list some of them: *Fat Seagulls Fall Over; Frog Stops Freightened Omnibus; Fraud Spuad Family Outing; Folk Society Fund Organiser; Family Saved From Octopus; Frigmund Seud Freaks Out; French Student Fails 'O' level; Free Shells for Oysters; Flowers Subdue Ferret Odour. By the end of the day they had already become collectors items and were even seen being worn at the Government House Garden Party.*

Two variations on the theme! Hazel Hannan, M.H.K., suggested the slogan should read Folk Society Fund Organiser. However, the badge above, which was found for sale, sported a different message.

Hazel Hannan, MHK, supporting FSFO.

Vannin continues to maintain its nationalistic purity of thought. However, the undeniable benefits of the finance sector are now acknowledged even by many nationalists.

Just as the concerns and protests of nationalists have successfully engendered a revival of interest in Manx identity, history and culture, perhaps ironically partly funded by the success of the finance sector, so the prosperity and openings generated by that sector have encouraged Manx people to remain in the Island or to return to it, in order to seize the opportunities offered by the thriving business community. They are now able to earn a good living on the Island, where there is virtually no unemployment. However the consequences of success in the development of the finance sector has produced results which have affected the physical appearance of the Island and which transformed the towns from holiday destinations to a business environment.[83]

CHAPTER 11

THE TRANSFORMATION OF THE LANDSCAPE

Housing Developments

Like those of its closest neighbours, Ireland, Wales and Scotland, to an extent not matched in England, the buildings of the Isle of Man have reflected the changing purposes and fluctuations of wealth through the succeeding ages. Until the eighteenth century, most Manx buildings were modest and utilitarian, taking the form of single-storey cottages or crofts, and occasional two-storey farmhouses with attendant farm buildings, often part of the residential structure. The exceptions were the two castles, Castle Rushen and Peel, Bishopscourt at Kirk Michael, residence of the Bishops of Sodor and Man, and the occasional residence of a prominent family, such as Milntown, Lezayre, which belonged to the powerful Christian clan. Most Manx churches, too, were small and simple before the programme of rebuilding during the second half of the eighteenth century.

The development of various kinds of economic activity provided the incentive and means for the building of grander dwellings (for example, Bridge House, Castletown; Kentraugh, Gansey; Kirby, Braddan) or the improvement of existing farmhouses through rebuilding or extension in the Georgian style (for example, Ballacosnahan and Farmhill). Similarly, there were developments in the Georgian style within towns for occupation by the new professional or official classes, such as the Crofts and Bowling Green Road in Castletown and Athol Street in Douglas. In the later phases substantial houses in the Regency style were being built on the outskirts of Douglas and Ramsey as late as the 1860s.

The dawn of the tourist trade saw more extensive development in the Victorian style, mostly in Douglas, but also along the seafronts of other towns and villages. The main period of construction was between the

The Grove, Peel. An attractive mixed development by Jonathan Irving's company, Street Heritage, modelled on some of Peel's older houses.

1880s and the outbreak of the Great War in 1914; very substantial terraced boarding houses were built along the Island's principal bays. Progressively smaller terraced houses away from the promenades were also largely used as boarding houses. Between the wars substantial development continued on open land, particularly in the Douglas area. Many of the houses, like those in Devonshire Road and Cronkbourne Road, were suburban villas in the Edwardian style or in the Arts and Crafts style introduced to the Island by Baillie Scott.

There was little building after the Second World War until the introduction of the New Residents policy. The economic factors encouraging building were largely lacking, and for a prolonged period restrictions made materials unavailable. The claim that in 1961 only one new house was built, symbolizing the decline of the economy and of the population, has already been referred to. However, contrary to the beliefs of those resolutely opposed to the expansion of the population and the resultant increase in housing, the process of expansion had already been going on in the Island for two hundred years. This is not to deny that finding suitable land for residential building and providing housing of suitable quality at affordable prices are major problems. But, as is the case

with so many protests against the increase in the numbers of new
residents and the expansion of the financial services sector, the
responsibility cannot be laid simply at the door of either. The demand for
housing does not stem uniquely from these new developments. Manx
people themselves contribute to the demand for better housing; families
who would formerly have occupied one household now want separate
accommodation, for matrimonial reasons, or because modern young
adults expect to have homes of their own. Countries like England and
Ireland have faced similar problems and have not dealt with them with
any greater measure of success.

Expansion

In 1960, at the time of the introduction of the New Residents policy,
the Island's housing stock was generally rundown; it was poorly
maintained and in need of paint and of limited attraction to potential new
residents. Some more substantial properties had already been acquired
and renovated by people who had arrived between the end of the war and
1960. Many of these new residents were of relatively modest means and
expectations, but even for these the burden of income tax and surtax in
the UK and the low level at which the highest rates started, together with
the threat of a confiscatory Labour government (which was in fact elected
in 1964), made the move to the Island an attractive prospect. Since the
end of the Second World War the Island had also seen an intermittent
influx of retired civil servants, farmers, professionals and businessmen,
particularly from Africa and the Caribbean and other parts of the rapidly
disappearing British Empire, and a few wealthier people, primarily from
England and the Irish Republic. All these categories of new residents
found the Island offered few homes which lived up to their dreams of
retirement in a charming English or Irish country house, or set in a
picturesque English village. These simply do not exist in the Island.

Before this sudden increase in demand there had been little need in
the Island for strategic development plans or experience in the detailed
control of development or of alterations to existing buildings. The
Victorian terraced houses of upper Douglas and elsewhere, a type of

Many Victorian houses and boarding houses in Upper Douglas were converted for modern residential use, such as these in Bradda Mount

housing that in London and other English cities even by this time was in demand for renovation or conversion, were almost entirely overlooked. Demand was met either by conversion of existing properties, mostly in the countryside, or by new developments on the outskirts of Douglas, Ramsey and Port Erin.

Many conversions rescued farm-houses and barns that were in poor repair and might well have fallen into ruin; most were sensitively undertaken both in scale and design without 'urbanizing' the countryside; many of the larger houses that were sold to new comers required modernization, and this was sympathetically achieved. This included the restoration of abandoned cottages in the countryside; such restorations were later severely restricted by the planners. Although initially ignored, some of the older urban properties too have since been attractively renovated. There have, of course, been less successful efforts[84]. But in general it must be said that the process has been of benefit, upgrading the quality of the Island's housing stock and enhancing its attractiveness.

However, a far as undesirable development is concerned, the principal offenders have been the larger development schemes at all price levels. Many of the early bungalow estates of north Ramsey and Port Erin were ill-designed and ill-constructed, and did not offer accommodation of a good standard. This urban sprawl, indiscriminate in its location, indifferent in its layout, design and quality, would certainly not have been permitted at a later date. In the early days there were also more expensive developments, more spaciously laid out, in more attractive locations, although it is likely that these sites, too, would not have received planning permission in the last twenty years. Examples of such developments are King Edward Road and the Booilushag estate in Maughold.

The passage of time has not solved the problems of development. In the 1980s the Planning Department produced a series of Strategic Plans designating areas where, prima facie, development will or will not be permitted; these plans are, at the time of writing, in the process of rather belated revision. Politicians stridently demand an increase in the availability of 'affordable' or 'first time buyer' housing. This could be provided by releasing large areas of land not at present zoned for housing development, since it is the shortage of building land which is to a great extent responsible for the high cost of housing. But such a step would be at the expense of the unspoiled Manx countryside.

This dilemma is common throughout the British Isles. One has only to consider Dublin and other Irish cities to understand that matters could easily be a great deal worse. In Ireland in the 1960s to 1980s there appeared to be a penchant for slab bungalows constructed from multicoloured concrete blocks; now the fashion has moved to over-ornamented 'Georgian' detached houses with decorative urban walls and gates; these have even invaded the countryside.

It is impossible to satisfy everyone: although the planners have had some success with the very difficult task of controlling development, they have not escaped criticism. Some of their decisions appear illogical, often in apparently trivial matters; more recently, the cost of planning

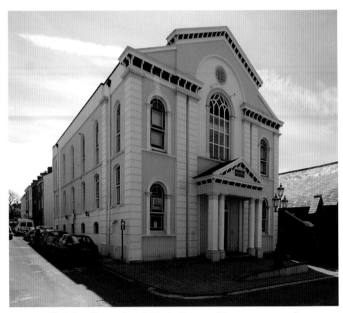

Christian Street chapel, Peel. Converted into apartments by
Street Heritage, as Chapel Court.

applications and the slow speed with which they are processed have caused discontent. There have also been some unexpected, perhaps inexplicable, outcomes in both major and minor schemes. The most notorious case is that of a development which, as first presented to the public, was for a hotel, sports facilities and golf course, with limited high quality housing for seasonal letting at Mount Murray, Santon, near Douglas, on the site of a disused entertainment facility, the Alex Inn. This development turned, virtually imperceptibly into a regular housing scheme for full-time occupation, many of the units being small terraced houses set incongruously in the heart of what had been partly rolling countryside. The explanation, revealed by two expensive Inquiries, showed what most people had always known from the start, namely, that the planning process had failed: it had not functioned as it was intended. This kind of thing cannot help but reduce public confidence in the impartiality, fairness and incorruptibility of the planning process, whether or not such lack of confidence is in fact justified.

The general dislike of development, developers and the planning process naturally hardened into hostility, at first towards new residents generally, and later towards the finance industry, both of which were blamed for despoiling the Isle of Man, an attitude to which the air of superiority assumed by certain comeovers contributed.

In the second stage, after the conversion of country properties and building of the first estates, bungalow development continued wherever possible, although the houses were perhaps of higher quality, and the builders were largely local. One developer in particular, Mill-Baldwin, attempted to improve the design of their new houses, initially only the larger houses, which were often embellished with columns or porticoes; this endeavour was subsequently extended to include smaller properties too. Whether the Georgianesque style was in keeping with the Island's architectural traditions is open to debate, bearing in mind the precedent of the Island's Regency villas of the mid 19th century; the appropriateness of the columns and pitch of the roofs can be questioned. Nevertheless, the houses were well-built and designed with care, and they fulfilled a need. Later developers who are still active have been criticized (whether fairly or not) both for over-development and quality of product; certainly some of the cramped developments, built from dark materials and liberally adorned with half-timber features, look out of place in the Manx landscape.

For a very long time, well into the 1980s, the Government's policy towards Douglas promenade was that it should be preserved in its entirety as the finest example of a Victorian seaside resort surviving in the British Isles. The Government persisted in the belief that the Island's tourist industry would recover, and the hotels would be needed. But by 1990 there had already been three significant breaches in the promenade's imposing *façade*. These were the Loch Promenade church replacement, the demolition of the Derby Castle complex and its replacement by Summerland, and the redevelopment of the Palace site to make way for the modern Palace Hotel and Casino under the terms of the Casino licence. The rest of the promenade was rigorously protected, despite the lack of demand for tourist accommodation. Even conversion to other uses, such

King's Court, Ramsey. The old streets of south Ramsey were destroyed for this development, built in 1974. It was, for fifteen years, the only major apartment building in the Island. The views from the flats are superb.

as offices or apartments was forbidden, although had it been permitted it might well have saved the appearance of the Victorian promenade, despite the poor structural quality of many of the Victorian buildings. Nevertheless, the delay may have hastened the end of the promenade's tourist appeal, as the unoccupied and shabby condition of many of the properties constituted a very poor advertisement for the Island.

Apartments

Eventually, some conversion to apartments was permitted, followed by permission to demolish the Grasmere and adjacent hotels to build purpose apartments, Queen's Mansions, in an alien Georgian style. These, some of the earliest purpose-built apartments in the Island, were very slow to sell, partly because of price, partly because of a reluctance in the Island to live in such apartments, and partly because they came on the market around 1990 when there was an obvious depression in the housing

"Hang on, I'll just finish washing the car"

Fo Halloo Free Manx Press cartoon.

market. However, after some delay, the appeal of apartments at the Queen's Promenade end of the bay strengthened, and there was widespread demolition of most of the older property. The newer apartments, of varying quality and architectural merit, reflect the Victorian styles of their demolished predecessors reasonably well.

The significant exception to this lack of apartments in the early period was the building in 1974 of the King's and Queen's Courts on the ruins of South Ramsey. By any standards these buildings were incongruous in appearance, if not downright ugly, and for almost twenty years they had no successors. However, the demand for apartments grew rapidly in the 1990s and into the new century, and there were schemes in Castletown, Ramsey, Port Erin and Port St Mary, mostly implemented through the demolition or conversion of former hotels. In addition, luxury developments were built on Onchan Head, the King Edward Bay Apartments on the site of the White City, and the Majestic Apartments on the site of Baillie Scott's Majestic Hotel (which the conservation

The Courthouse, Douglas. Opened in the 1990s to replace the old courthouse in Athol Street, it has not been without problems. A firm of Edinburgh architects was commissioned to design it. The new Deeds Registry is on the left.

movement failed to save). Ironically, conservation societies have often made things worse by their uncompromising stance. For example, the Forresters (*sic*) Arms in St George's Street in Douglas was to be modernized internally using two adjacent houses, all dating from the 1860s, in an unbroken block of streetscape, in the way favoured by pubs for ease of operation; this would have involved sweeping away certain internal features dating only from the 1930s, and the proposal inspired a spirited and misguided campaign for total registration mounted by the Victorian Society, CAMRA and other bodies. By the time this had been dealt with the brewery had made provision elsewhere. In 2006 the building had become unsafe and was demolished.

Much of the recent development has been in the form of houses for working families, and has consumed ever larger tracts of land in Braddan, Onchan, Peel and Port Erin. The latest initiative, offering an income tax cap of £100,000, has already attracted interest, but has also demonstrated the dearth of property which would appeal to this level of wealth. It will be interesting to observe how the authorities cope with these current demands.

Commercial Buildings

A similar process of change had affected buildings used for commercial purposes such as conversion for office use or others newly built for that purpose. The process was to transform the centre of Douglas.

Athol Street had begun a move from residential use back in the late nineteenth century. Advocates and other professionals had moved their offices into the Street's elegant terraces; by 1894 the first firm of chartered accountants on the Island, W. H. Walker & Co (now PKF) had set up its offices in number 50 Athol Street, where the firm was to remain for 100 years. The Isle of Man Bank had established its head office on the corner of Athol Street and Prospect Hill. By 1960 Athol Street provided premises for numerous firms of advocates, two firms of stockbrokers, Tower Insurance, Commercial Union, as well as other businesses. At the time it was the hub of the Island's financial and professional life earning it the dubious description as 'the only street in the world to be shady on both sides'.[85]

The abolition of surtax in 1960 was designed to attract new residents, so for the first few years the limited immediate effect on demand for office space was satisfied by the conversion of residential property in Douglas town centre. However, it became apparent that there would be a demand for purpose-built offices, and a group of buildings comprising a hotel and old shops on Prospect Hill was demolished in 1972 to erect the first phase of Victory House, in an uncompromisingly modern style, but plain and without architectural pretensions. It could however be argued that such absence of architectural pretension is preferable to the sort of monstrosity exhibited by Murray House with its barbaric fibreglass stick-on Ionic pilasters, incorrect in every particular. It is a nice irony that the offices of the Island's planning department can be found within.

Victory House was followed, at regular intervals during the 1970s, by Exchange House in Athol Street and the new Government Offices adjacent to Tynwald, neither particularly well-designed for modern use, nor of any architectural distinction. These two factors, of basic unattractive appearance and limited use, particularly in view of the paucity of air and light and the absence of facilities and space for modern

Murray House, Douglas. The fibreglass columns are slapped on the front without any feeling for their Ionic models, especially in the barbaric misunderstanding of the capitals. It is one of the most architecturally illiterate buildings in the Island. Ironically, it houses the Planning Department.

ducting, were to bedevil many of the new offices. Some of the new developments involved the loss of important buildings or groups of buildings, for instance, the new Barclays branch, which replaced a magnificent Methodist church in Victoria Street, and the iconic, if ugly, Postal Sorting Office in Circular Road. Indeed, much of Circular Road, a street of little architectural distinction, was to give way to a series of offices. Architects clearly were struggling to find a coherent style for new offices, but in common with other cities have produced a wide variety of differing contributions.

There were various schemes of renovation and replacement in a similar style. Amongst these were the renovation and restoration by Cains on the corner of Athol Street and lower Church Street, pairs of old Athol Street buildings combined and restored by Ramsey Crookall & Co, Close

Brothers, Fidelta Trust and Quinn Kneale, the terrace on the north side of lower St George's Street, the conversion into offices for Simcocks of the old Ridgeway Hotel in Victoria Street, and the conversion of the Jubilee Building previously containing Noble's Baths, Yates' Wine Lodge and the Regal Cinema. The interiors, if they were still in existence, were largely lost, and extensions were added behind the buildings to make full use of the ground space, but the frontage was maintained or enhanced.

Much building activity took place in the late 1980s and 1990s, largely of a speculative nature, without specific occupiers in mind, in response to an anticipated increase in demand, an expectation which was usually fulfilled. Many of these edifices were free-standing and include some of the more striking additions to the Douglas streetscape: mention can be made of the Royal Skandia Life building on the site of the Douglas Bay Hotel, the grandiose, classical headquarters of Coutts in Onchan, and the DOHLE offices high above Douglas harbour which successfully recalled the style and shape of the much-loved Fort Anne Hotel, long since demolished.

The majority of the new offices were in Douglas; Ramsey had a few, and in the South, convenient for the airport, Ballasalla and Castletown saw some conversions, like Lorne House and St Mary's garrison church, and some new buildings, notably what was originally the headquarters of Royal and Sun Alliance International.

Traffic Problems

All these new offices, as well as the rise of population and general prosperity, brought a huge increase in the number of cars. Increasingly, planners had allowed for parking spaces in consideration of planning approval, but this was not sufficient to cater for the demand; long gone were the days when the good wives of Douglas parked in Strand Street for as long as they pleased, to do their shopping and take coffee with their friends. Castle/Strand/Duke Streets had been pedestrianized; double yellow lines were introduced, together with a scheme for disc parking.[86] Four multi-storey car parks were built, two of which were further extended, in Shaw's Brow, Chester Street, above Marks & Spencer and on the site of Mylchreests Motors.

None of these enhances the beauty of Douglas, but they are reasonably well concealed. People's reluctance to use public transport for commuting and shopping, or to pay for a parking space, compounds the problem and two of the less attractive features of Douglas during the day are workers' habits of parking just outside the controlled area, in residential districts, and the waltz of vehicles moving every two hours when the time limits on discs expire. (The other, exceedingly unattractive sight, common throughout Europe, is that of workers lurking in garage basements or cowering, whatever the weather, in the front or back doors of premises to have a quick fag).

In the end, offices did spread to the promenade, firstly when the Peveril Hotel opposite the Sea Terminal was demolished to provide a headquarters for Lloyds TSB International, and when the block containing the Villiers Hotel was demolished, and in due course partly redeveloped to become the headquarters of the Royal Bank of Scotland International, leaving incongruous voids on either side. The building is in an uncompromisingly modern style that seems to have obtained planning approval through crafty architectural drawings. Such unfinished business will be of interest in the future, as will be the quest for alternative uses for all these new offices, should the financial services sector cease to flourish.

Another aspect of all this construction activity is the importance of the construction industry to the Manx economy and employment.[87] A downturn in construction makes itself felt and the failure to provide enough houses has a serious effect on house prices.[88] Looking ahead, the prospect is for the spread of more suburban sprawl into the countryside, and more redevelopment for offices in and around Douglas.

It has been interesting to note that, even in the circumstances of the 2007/08 world banking crises, when many house prices in the UK have fallen, interest rates have risen and mortgages proved harder to obtain, house prices in the Isle of Man have proved remarkably steady and demand for new houses has continued.[89]

CHAPTER 12

BUT MAN I S AN ISLAND

As will be apparent, Man is not only an island but a distinct jurisdiction; this has served it well for three centuries in various different ways. Man may be an island, but it needs to work and interact with its neighbours; until recently, Man interrelated chiefly with other parts of the British Isles, its immediate neighbours, but today its relationships extend to Europe and far beyond. Such relationships can only be successful so long as the Isle of Man is known to offer services of the highest quality.

The early days of Man's development as a financial centre were marked by a few teething troubles: there was the resistance of local people to change, their suspicion of new enterprises and new residents culminating in the protests orchestrated by *Fo Halloo* and *FSFO*. There was some justification for the protesters' concern: development did pose a threat to Manx identity, the Island's environment, and its reputation. But in some respects the protesters' attitude was unrealistic: human beings, however altruistic or idealistic they may be, share certain basic needs: the need for food, clothing, healthcare and education; all these come at a price. The Island's traditional industries, agriculture, fishing, tourism, and the recent small manufacturing sector, would never have been able to provide the economic basis to fund a modern lifestyle. Large numbers of Manx-born young people were forced to seek employment off the Island. The modernization and replacement of the Island's infrastructure and utilities - water, sewers, gas, electricity, ports (and airport), roads, schools and hospital, many of these installations over a hundred years old - was long overdue. Upgrading would have had to happen irrespective of increases in population, but there would not have been the money to pay for it. Nor could the Island have avoided the increasing costs of healthcare, education and welfare on a scale hard to predict back in 1960.

A cursory glance around the Island today reveals the level of investment that has been made; without the economic contribution of new residents and new enterprises this could only have been achieved by means of external subsidy which might have resulted in the Island's absorption into the United Kingdom, with consequent loss of its independence.

The collapse of the Savings and Investment Bank in 1982 rocked the Island and shocked its politicians; for a while, it made the Island an international laughing-stock. At the same time it dramatically increased awareness of the Island's potential. It also alerted the Manx authorities to the need to ensure quality of services. The consequent improvement has meant that the history of the Island's economic activities has been much more stable, if less colourful, since the SIB fiasco.

Politically the period has been marked by two developments, internal and external. Internally, there has been the steady devolution of power from the UK and the Queen's representative, the Lieutenant Governor, to Tynwald, and the House of Keys in particular. In 1987 the twenty-four Boards of Tynwald, with extensively overlapping membership, were subsumed into new Ministries presided over by Ministers who collectively constituted the Council of Ministers, presided over in turn by the Chief Minister, who is elected by Tynwald. The advantages of this system are self-evident; it makes 'joined-up government' possible in a way that was not possible under the Board system. Most ordinary members of Tynwald are involved as members of one or more departments; this offers useful experience and involvement in government, but perhaps makes members less able to stand back and review developments with a constructively critical eye. The numerical dominance of the nine members of the Council of Ministers, in addition to the wide participation of other Tynwald members in government, makes it difficult for an impartial viewpoint to be maintained; those members who do criticise are often perceived as petty and self-serving, eager to promote themselves rather than the good of the Island. The situation is compounded by an almost universal reluctance on the part of members of the House of Keys to allow the Legislative Council to fulfil its proper role, that of protecting the Manx people against the effects of potential excesses by the Keys. The fear of an alternative source of power makes members unwilling either to approve an acceptable form of direct election to the Council, or to widen the pool of talent through the existing system of election. The bungling attempts to fill the last place on the Council in the Spring of 2007 and again in 2008 demonstrated a disconcerting lack of constitutional understanding in a number of members of the Keys; the proposal, by Victor Kneale[90] and David Cannan[91] for an election of 32 members and subsequent division demonstrates a lack of appreciation of the important distinct function of the Council. Members were, however, content to retain the undemocratic voting system with constituencies of different size, although Victor Kneale's proposal for the reintroduction of the single transferable vote, or David Cannan's, for constituencies of equal size, would offer the only fair and equitable solutions.

Nevertheless, the policies of successive Chief Ministers and their teams have been surprisingly consistent; the declared aim has been the 'Development of a Prosperous and Caring Society'. Critics would object that this aim is bland, and claim that it has not been achieved. Clearly, there are glaring inequalities, and that will be true in even the most perfect Socialist Elysium, should such exist; unforeseen events will produce problems; Government will be unable to provide a panacea.

With regard to external relations, there has been significant development, from the considerable devolution of power under the Isle of Man Act of 1958, to the surrender of the executive function of the Lieutenant Governor in the time of Sir John Paul (1974-80), and the transfer of most of the remaining constitutional functions of the Lieutenant Governor in the time of Sir Laurence New (1985-90) to directly elected members of the Keys; after this date the Lieutenant Governor's chief function was to act as representative of the Queen as Head of State, and to hold limited emergency powers; his remaining roles are symbolic and social. Other important developments occurred during this period, chief amongst them perhaps the accession of the United Kingdom to the European Economic Community under the Treaty of Rome, to which the three dependencies in the British Isles were appended by Protocol 3; this was, on the whole, greatly to the Islands' advantage. The Isle of Man maintains strong links with the UK through its reciprocal arrangements for social security and pensions and the National Health Service, and the Customs and Excise Agreement, although this has undergone some modifications over time. Also, in addition to the long-standing double tax agreement with the UK made in 1955, the Island has more recently entered into a series of more limited tax agreements with a number of countries including the USA, Australia, Ireland and Denmark, and is discussing similar agreements with India and China; twelve agreements were in place by January 2009. It remains important for the Island when dealing with the UK and outside world, to co-operate with Jersey and Guernsey, with which jurisdictions the Island has much in common.

The Island's legislation has from time to time been out of step with that of the United Kingdom, and therefore with that of Europe, on matters relating to Human Rights, capital punishment, birching, and sexual relations. There has also been a sense that the UK Government, as the Island's protective power, has not always shown due care for the welfare of those of its dependencies which are to some degree in competition with it. This is an old grudge which has characterised the Island's relationship with the United Kingdom since Revestment; conversely, it is hardly surprising that the islands do not rank high in the priorities of Westminster. Until the introduction of ministerial government in the Island in 1986 there had been a standing committee to deal with the UK, chaired by Sir Charles Kerruish; its transactions were characterised by ill-concealed hostility towards the UK. The committee was discontinued after 1987 and its role taken over by the Chief Minister and others, with, according to them, greater harmony and success.

It should be acknowledged, however, that all the evidence suggests that recently the British Government has generally been consistently supportive of development and constitutional change in the Island, in cases where it can be shown that the various proposals have the support of the people.[92] All the Island's Chief Ministers (or equivalent) have conceded, in conversation, that the United Kingdom has been supportive and that they have enjoyed good relations with the Home Office or Department of Constitutional Affairs. During the SIB crisis, the Bank of England, which had experienced far worse problems only eight years previously, provided extremely helpful advice. The Bank also provided the services of R H Farrant and W M Hyde in 1982 to examine the situation after the collapse and make recommendations, and almost certainly to assist in the matter of the recruitment of a banking supervisor. During the change to ministerial government there was no interference.

Each successive Chief Minister up to the present day has acknowledged the good relationship with the British Government. There is, in consequence, no deep-seated desire, either on the part of politicians or of the general public, to move away from the Island's current status of Crown Dependency. This could of course change, if the UK were either unwilling or unable to defend the Island from threats emanating from the European Union, perhaps as a result of a new treaty or a new constitution in which the Island's relationship with the EU should once more be put in question. The announcement in May 2007 of a new ten point declaration, signed by the Chief Minister and the Lord Chancellor, clarifying the Island's independent requirements nationally and internationally, has confirmed recognition of the Island's status.

One of the threats to all jurisdictions is that of excessive regulation and interference, not only in daily life but in the conduct of business. The motives for such interference vary, but the excuse that is usually offered is the increase in terrorist and criminal activity. The most pervasive and invasive proposal by the British Government to date is the introduction of identity cards; but most people already encounter over-zealous officialdom whenever they pass through airports, open bank accounts, and so on. In these times of Political Correctness, people have to watch what they say in case a chance remark might be interpreted as sexist, racist, ageist, or in other ways offensive to particular susceptibilities. Health and Safety has become another area which impinges, often, it would seem, unnecessarily or even absurdly, upon normal life or business; people are becoming increasingly resentful of these intrusions into their private lives. The European Union seems addicted to making rules and issuing directives to which only the Northern Europeans - the British, Germans, and Scandinavians, appear to pay any attention, while they are blithely ignored by the Mediterranean nations. Petty officials, whether in government or institutions such as banks, seem to delight in enforcing these rules and regulations to the letter; possibly they are unable to discern the purpose behind the rules and may lack the judgement to interpret them judiciously and flexibly. The 'blame' culture, which encourages people to rush into litigation for the redress of any grievance, real or perceived, does not help, causing those responsible for implementing the rules to develop an obsession with covering their own backs.

As far as the Island is concerned, the question is to what extent it is free to pick and choose which rules it introduces. With due vigilance it may be able to avoid importing unnecessary over-regulation. But too often, rather than considering wisely, the Manx Government, spurred on by certain members of Tynwald, hastens to follow its larger neighbours; one example (without entering into a debate on the intrinsic merits of the case) is the anti-smoking law, a clear intrusion into individuals' private and legal way of life. But Man is an Island, and its Government needs to use its discretion and take advantage of its position.

Sometimes the Isle of Man appears to get it right and lead the way, as in the recent and on the whole successful relaxation of the licensing laws. Other absurdities introduced in England have so far been avoided, for example, the imposition of Home Information Packs for selling houses, which include 'thermal efficiency'; there is now a proposal to extend this system to rental property, renewable every three years, at an estimated cost of hundreds of pounds. Legislators would do well to bear in mind the dictum of the great Adam Smith: 'The proposal of any new law or regulation of commerce..... ought always to be listened to with great precaution..... It comes from an order of men..... who have generally an interest to deceive and even to oppress the public'.

The Manx Government's general lack of confidence and the personal hobby-horses of individual members of Tynwald are responsible for many of the more irritating changes that have occurred. This combination of diffidence and obsession has led to the appointment at vast expense of so-called 'consultants', who in many cases start out knowing little more about the subject of their studies than those who hire them. These consultants' reports are often bland and devoid of any useful recommendations; in many cases the answers they produce should have been self-evident to those who commissioned them. But commissioning consultants' reports enables the authorities to defer the awful moment of decision, and, when it can be deferred no longer, the reports provide some kind of 'crutch' to silence critics. Similarly, the modern cry for an Enquiry into various contentious issues, which is not confined to the Isle of Man, is often no more than a sop to appease vociferous critics; in the case of the two Mount Murray enquiries,[93] for instance, the reports produced answers that were for the most part common knowledge, involving reduplication of effort and great expense, merely to satisfy the obsession of one individual politician who claimed to speak for the Manx people.

In the forty-eight years since the abolition of surtax, the statistics in respect of both government revenue and personal wealth have for the most part shown remarkable progress. Average personal wealth can be measured by GDP figures per caput (Appendix C). The Island's low unemployment figures show that jobs are available for those willing to work; furthermore, although working off-Island might develop their skills and experience, it is no longer necessary for young Manx people to leave the Island in order to obtain reasonable, all year employment. The balance of population between Manx (however defined) and non-Manx continues to be a potential problem, but the work-permit legislation, though not designed for the purpose, serves as a brake on indiscriminate immigration and does so with fewer side-effects and over-protection of natives than the arrangements in, for example, Bermuda or the Caymans. Proposals under the control of residence legislation are potentially intrusive and divisive and could well have unintended consequences; such proposals with suitable modifications may be best reserved for emergencies.

Governments always need to be vigilant to curb unnecessary expenditure. They can never do everything they may wish to, and in any case, as Professor Parkinson remarked when he lived here, they should perhaps confine their activities to what they alone can do. Those MHKs who believe that government is like a business, raising more money in order to spend it, are dangerously mistaken. The policy introduced in the time of Miles Walker[94] and David Cannan, of setting aside surplus revenue as a reserve rather than treating it as funds available for expending, has served the Island well and strengthened it against the possibility of harder times. Governments may decide to support from their revenues a wide range of services, such as health, education, social security, pensions, cultural support, roads, police and so on; there are other activities which could be self-financing, such as power, water, ports and airport. However, even those activities that are funded by government do not have to be provided by government employees. Electricity, water, and road building and maintenance could be carried out by detached bodies even if they were established by Government; even the health and education services could revert to the position of self-funding trusts contracting to provide services at an agreed price. These suggestions were included in the 'Review of the Scope and Structure of Government' by Robert Quayle, former Clerk of Tynwald, Fred Kissack, former Government Secretary, and Sir Miles Walker, former Chief Minister, published in September 2006; the current Chief Minister and Government have shown little inclination to adopt them.

In 2006/07 Government expenditure was estimated by then at £769m, by far the largest portion of which, £374m, was spent on health, and £95m on education; these sectors employed 37% and 24% of the Government work force respectively. The proportion of the workforce employed in the business of government was 16.24%, compared with Bermuda at 10.4%, and the share of GDP spent by Government in 2004/05 came to the high proportion of 47.2%. Any move to reduce the disproportionately large number of employees on the Government pay-roll merits serious consideration, but it would require vision and willpower to achieve it. To this end, the mechanics of government need refining and if possible, trimming down. The senior civil servants within the ministries should be well-qualified people able to take responsibility and exercise it in a wise and consistent manner. They should be capable of advising their ministers from time to time on the policy matters that require their decision, and of running their own departments efficiently. In the 1990s such leaders were emerging out of the old board system, but the process needs to be resolutely encouraged. Inefficiency in those who hold senior positions cannot be tolerated. When necessary, the appropriate people should be recruited off-Island. A competent Civil Service is fundamental to the success of government.

Various public surveys have revealed that, by and large, the Island's inhabitants are satisfied with their quality of life. One survey was carried out during Miles Walker's time as Chief Minister, and another more recently, in connexion with the branding exercise that produced the slogan 'Freedom to Flourish' to sum up what the Island has to offer. General satisfaction formed part of the basis on which that slogan was founded. That is not to say that there is not widespread concern and dissatisfaction about development and developers, particularly when those developers seem able to dominate the decision-making process and obtain favourable rulings that are clearly at odds with public opinion, and which threaten sensitive areas and the landscape generally. If the developers could produce an ample supply of reasonably-priced houses, not only luxury homes, they might find acceptance. But the present situation is not regarded as acceptable. Government's planning department faces some hard decisions; too often its rulings come over as ineffectual or even capricious, obsessed with petty detail, and the process itself is unconscionably slow. As in the 1970s there are still some Manx land-owners who are willing to sell off their land, especially in beautiful locations, to speculative developers; there are developers who use repeated planning applications as a ploy to wear down the organization and resistance of groups of concerned citizens who care about the environment. The continuing battle over coastal land at Scarlett, an area of natural beauty near Castletown in the South, and what is perceived by many to be the attempted demolition of the centre of historic Castletown, are good examples of these skirmishes.

All these observations are intended to draw attention to the crucial issues which need to be considered and dealt with, whatever the future holds. The Island has considerable scope to survive and prosper so long as it is able to foresee threats and seize opportunities. Hitherto, it has, on the whole, managed to do this successfully even if much of this success has been more a question of reaction to events as they have unfolded than foresight. In the future more skill may be needed to predict developments; contingency plans to deal with eventualities and potential dangers should be at the heart of Government thinking, even if not publicly disclosed. Such plans would need to deal with threats to the Island's independence of action, to its products and activities and its taxation policies which make it a low-tax financial services jurisdiction. Big states and international bodies dislike smaller ones and would gladly see them stripped of the right to set their own policies and even to exist. But the position is illogical: where are they to draw the line? The American administration's handling of the Iraq crisis affords small grounds for confidence in its ability to deal appropriately with client or dependent states. The Isle of Man needs to have in place alternative strategies which are not hasty *ad hoc* solutions but well thought-out plans, perhaps going so far as to embrace complete independence, despite the disadvantages and the present popular disinclination for such a solution.

In the meantime the principal achievements of recent years have been the stability of Government finances and the quality of the services, financial or otherwise, which the Island provides. The SIB collapse was a catalyst without which the Government might well not have put in place the people and measures that were needed. All the Chief Ministers (and their equivalent), Treasury Ministers and regulators have emphasized the vital importance of quality. The Edwards Report and IMF visits identified this quality in the Island's financial services. The Island has much to build on and to promote; it can prove beyond a doubt that it has the quality, the enterprise and the independence of mind to withstand threats, irrespective of where they may come from, the EU, the United States, or even the UK.

Over the past half-century the Island has begun to show that despite mistakes and blemishes, it has developed in every way from a sleepy, underprivileged, old-fashioned, if pleasant enough, backwater, to a leader in the field in many areas of modern endeavour. To its neighbours and to the world at large, let it be known that Man is indeed 'an Island, entire of itself, and also a piece of the Continent, a part of the main'.[95]

CHAPTER 13

OR IS IT? - A POSTSCRIPT

The text of the book as written in 2007 ended with an optimistic note, applauding the Island's achievements outlining the success in maintaining quality of services and regulation which was approved both by the IMF and the British Government in the form of the Edwards report. And then it experienced the shock of the collapse of Iceland (ironically its counterpart as a surviving Viking jurisdiction) and of its banks.

On 8th October 2008 the British Government seized or froze the assets of Icelandic owned banks which were within the United Kingdom, by using a Treasury Sanction under provisions of Section 14 of the Terrorism Act 2000. The immediate effect, as far as the Island was concerned, was that Kaupthing Singer and Friedlander (Isle of Man) had its main asset of £555m deposited in London with its fellow subsidiary of the Icelandic Kaupthing bank frozen immediately, out of total deposits of £821m by 8168 customers. In consequence the Manx subsidiary became insolvent in the sense that it could not meet its immediate liabilities, and the same day its Isle of Man banking licence was suspended. The following day, the directors of the bank perforce applied to the Court to have the bank put into voluntary liquidation and Michael Simpson of PricewaterhouseCoopers was appointed provisional liquidator.

The Treasury Minister immediately proposed an extension of the Depositors' Compensation Scheme to cover £50,000 of deposits by any individual, but this did not extend to companies, trusts or charities. It appeared at first that these would not even be covered under the old scheme up to £15,000 (three quarters of £20,000), but, after consideration by Tynwald, they too were to be covered up to £20,000.

There was much anger among depositors, many of whom were likely to lose considerable sums, and some of whom were charities including Hospice Care with over £1m on deposit which it had already instructed to be moved. Manx banks also were very unhappy, since they would be asked

Tony Brown, MHK, Chief Minister.

to contribute each year up to £500,000 (later reduced to £350,000) until the compensation was paid. Clearly this could take a number of years during which depositors were waiting for their limited compensation, or the proceeds of the remaining assets which theoretically amount to £266m, or 32% of their deposits. Of these, £195m were deposited with Kaupthing Bank in Iceland, leaving only £71m unconnected with Kaupthing. At the hearing of the adjourned petition on 27th November 2008, the provisional liquidator reported that £103m had been recovered. The hearing was adjourned for a further 60 days till 22nd January 2009 pending efforts to resolve the legalities or seek a purchaser of the bank. In the meantime, Tynwald had voted to contribute £150m of taxpayers' money to the compensation scheme, but this would not be activated until the liquidation was set in motion by the appointment of a liquidator. However, the attempt to establish the validity and amounts of claims by depositors pending this appointment, and communication with depositors were slow and unrevealing of the situation.

Allan Bell, MHK, Treasury Minister.

In the meantime a number of urgent steps had been taken. The Chief Minister, Tony Brown, and Allan Bell, Treasury Minister, had been to London to try to enlist the aid of the British Government in putting pressure on Iceland to release funds, perhaps by putting conditions on a proposed IMF loan to Iceland. Kaupthing Bank had itself instructed lawyers to consider action against the British Government for freezing the funds. Legal action was also being contemplated by individual depositors against the British Government for release of the funds, as well as against the FSC. Both John Aspden, head of the FSC, and Mike Simpson had visited Iceland to get them to honour the strong letter to comfort, almost a guarantee, from the parent bank to its Manx subsidiary. But no definite progress appeared to have been made by the time when, on 27th November 2008, the hearing was adjourned in the hope that some progress would be made.

To add to the problem for the Island, some depositors not unreasonably had been blaming the British seizure of the assets for their own loss of deposits and demanding compensation. At a meeting of the UK Treasury Select Committee in early November, the Chancellor of the Exchequer, Alistair Darling, sought to divert attention from his own role in causing the collapse of the Manx bank by attacking the depositors for evading British taxes. It could clearly be the case that some depositors are still not declaring their income to the UK or other tax authorities who have a legal right to tax it, but they are by now a small minority of total deposits and are already suffering a tax deduction under the EU Savings Tax Directive which removes much of the attraction of concealment. But to say what he is reported to have said reveals a gross and malicious misunderstanding of the UK's dependant territories, as if the problem would go away if they were suppressed and not simply pass to other independent territories, such as Switzerland or Singapore, outside the scope of any British influence or economic use of their assets. His remarks included 'Having looked at what has happened over the last few months, we really do need to have a long, hard look about the relationship between this country and the Isle of Man, a tax haven sitting in the Irish Sea. We've come to the situation where you have sitting there all sorts of tax advantages accruing to being in the Isle of Man, and, when things go wrong people then say what about the British compensation scheme.' Which it was not, but about repaying seized assets to the bank, not compensation to individuals. After a reaction from the Chief Minister, who wrote to the Chancellor and sought an urgent meeting with the Lord Chancellor to 'countermand' the 'ill-informed' comments, the Treasury commented 'the Chancellor was not talking about the constitutional relationship. He was talking about people's confusion about banking regulation and their expectation of protection for their savings....... What he said was quite clear; to say this is a constitutional issue is slightly over-blown.'

There is a real problem for all financial centres, as there is with banks. Iceland has demonstrated that its three banks had far outgrown the resources of their country to rescue them with its small economy of 300,000 inhabitants. But these banks had, in varying degrees, used depositors' money to make commercial acquisitions of trading and manufacturing companies, which has not recently been the case with most 'offshore' banks. As recent events have shown, as demonstrated vividly by the collapse in the exchang rate of the pound, even the United Kingdom cannot easily manage th problems arising from the collapse of financial systems.

The consequence has been that, to justify the Chancellor's remarks, the British government has appointed yet another Reviewer of offshore territories, Michael Foot, who was formerly managing director of the UK Financial Services Authority. He is to review all British dependencies with significant financial sectors to include the Island, the Channel Islands, Gibraltar, Cayman Islands, Bermuda, Virgin Islands and Turks and Caicos. In the meantime the IMF produced a draft report of its inspection in September 2008 which made certain suggestions for tightening up anti-money laundering procedures which were dealt with by Tynwald in December 2008. On 22nd April 2009 Michael Foot issued a progress report, showing no great cause for concern, especially since the Island, in common with other jurisdictions including several major national governments, was included in a 'white list' of compliant jusidictions in advance of the G 20 Summit held in April 2009. Quite what that means is not clear, but obviously it is better than being on the 'Black List' (of four jurisdictions) or on the 'Grey List' of countries yet to become compliant. However, Foot does make the point about smaller jurisdictions having protential problems if the large scale of their financial services is compared with the small size of their national economies, as in the case of Iceland.

Apart from the events already described, a number of pertinent questions arise. Did the FSC give a false sense of security by letting it be thought that the events of SIB and BCCI could not recur due to insistence that a material part of a licensed bank's liquidity should be placed outside the bank's group, and with the words 'Licensed by the Financial Supervision Commission'? It is true that the circumstances of Kaupthing's collapse were due to the arbitrary actions of sovereign governments rather than improvidence and fraud (SIB) or international fraud (BCCI). There was no such suggestion here, but even so was the amount deposited outside the group, which appears to be only £71m or only 8.6%, even an adequate insurance or indeed misleading to depositors relying on prudent supervision? What was the use of the parent company's guarantee, or the insistence of the transfer of £555m to the fellow Kaupthing subsidiary in the UK? If the FSC was to insist on a higher proportion of deposits outside a banking group, how many banks would close their operations in the Island? How many will go if they have to produce £350,000 compensation for several years? What would happen if a second bank got into difficulties, bearing in mind the limits to the Isle of Man's resources? It has to be said that the same questions are pertinent to all small financial jurisdictions, and that Jersey has no depositors' compensation scheme and Guernsey only a putative one. Ireland has a scheme but not so far made final, and there is doubt as to whether it can afford it.

A further question arises for the non-executive directors of Kaupthing. Donald Gelling, the chairman, is chairman of the Insurance and Pensions Authority and the former chief minister; John Cashen is vice chairman of the FSC and formerly a highly respected head of Treasury. There is a real question as to whether, despite relevant declarations of interest, they should be on those authorities and be directors of banks. However, in a small jurisdiction, it is not easy to find competent members of these authorities who have no continuing interests in directorships, for which it is equally difficult to find suitable candidates. The alternatives may be experienced people who are not so competent, or alternatively people of advanced years. And the role of Commissioner of the FSC requires considerable time, skill and decisiveness. The Kaupthing directors were presiding over the same problem faced by the FSC; on the face of it the bank was prudently run and solvent, but a larger amount than was comfortable was required to be placed with the group; which got into trouble as a consequence of a very unusual series of events.

There is another important question which affects in the first instance the United Kingdom but which is a lesson to all parliaments which give legal powers to governments, and that is in the use or misuse of sweeping powers. It is clear to the ordinary citizen that the Terrorism Act 2000 was intended to allow governments to act swiftly and decisively in dealing with the sort of international terrorism which has been increasingly frequent since its enactment. But how the troubles afflicting Iceland and its banks fall within its intended scope does not seem obvious to anyone except those who apply it. An even more recent example of the misuse of the Act and of the police squad trained to deal with terror incidents, to raid the house of the member of Parliament Damien Green, search it and arrest him, and then to search his office in the House of Commons without a warrant, on suspicion of having obtained information about illegal immigrants in security jobs from a civil servant, has sounded alarms; and this within a democratic and parliamentary system. This government's desire to use the threat of terrorism to increase the time during which the police can hold suspects to 42 days (are the powers confined to suspected terrorism) and to impose on every resident of the UK the requirement to carry an ID card loaded with personal information are further examples of this alarming and authoritarian tendency. And one only had to consider the government's handling of the decision to invade Iraq and the refusal to allow a referendum on the new EU treaty establishing a new quasi-constitution to be further disturbed.

Two other matters have disturbed the good working relations with the UK. Firstly notice was given by the UK that the reciprocal arrangements to use each other's National Health Service in each other's countries would cease, probably in 2010. This will create enormous problems especially for elderly people or those with medical conditions who may not be able to obtain travel insurance to visit friends or relations in the UK, or for those visiting the Island from the UK, and could not afford to fall ill without it. Why the UK government should take this unilateral act against the Isle of Man for what is likely to be small savings is not clear. But it gives the impression of a large neighbour bullying a smaller one. Secondly, in a vain attempt to revive a sluggish UK economy which was suffering from the effects not only of a world credit crisis but from the imprudence of Gordon Brown and Alistair Darling in spending the UK's resources, largely with little benefit to show for it, the Chancellor inter alia cut VAT from 17½ % to 15% for a period of 13 months from 1st December 2008 at a loss to the Island's revenues of what is estimated to be some £40m. Luckily Allan Bell has been more prudent in the handling of the Manx economy.

   This book will not be able to describe the outcome of all these new developments which may take some time, even many years. The recent events do not seem to invalidate the conclusions of the preceeding chapter, allowing the Island to be itself despite the buffets of fortune in an uncertain world.

REFERENCE NOTES

1   For the latest assessment of the Viking period and Tynwald, see Wilson D.M. *Vikings in the Isle of Man.*

2   Surtax, often called 'supertax', is a tax levied on incomes in excess of a certain figure, paid in addition to, but separate from, the ordinary income tax.

3   See appendix A

4   See appendix C

5   See Quilliam: 1989: 21 and *Proceedings of IOMNHAS* vol X No.4 317ff

6   Wilkins: 1999

7   Moore: 1977:437

8   'A quiet Retreat for Debtors', *The Manx Society*, Vol. XXI

9   Bullock: 1816: chapters 17 & 18

10   Stowell, J. A Ballad for the *Young Ladies and Gentlemen of Douglas Manx Merry Myths* 1875. J.Brown & Son, Douglas

11   Woods, G. *An Account of the Past and Present State of the Isle of Man*, 1811, London.

12   Crumplin, T., and Rawcliffe, R., *A Time of Manx Cheer*, Chapter 4

13   *Proceedings of IOMNHAS* XI No 2.

14   *3rd Interim Report of the Select Committee of Tynwald appointed to revise advocates' fees*

15   Birch J. W. :1964:126.

16   Birch: 1964:p 126

17   See Appendix A

18   See Appendix B

19   Tynwald 21 June 1960 Budget Debate

20   Tynwald 21 June 1960 : Budget Debate

21   Charles Kerruish said: 'when it fails, as it undoubtedly will'.

22   See Appendix A

23   The Isle of Man at 227 square miles is almost exactly the land area of Singapore (222 square miles before reclamation). Singapore supports some 4.5 million inhabitants.

24   The author was present on this occasion

25   See Chapter 10. In 2007, Binstock was ranked 700th in the *Times* 'Rich List', with a fortune of £100 million.

26   *Manx Star* 26-31 March 1973. In the same issue of the *Manx Star*, the call to nationalize estate agents is recorded. Although estate agents, like developers, are not often loved, it is hard to see what such a move was expected to achieve.

27   *Proceedings of IOMNHAS* Vol XI No. 2, based on an account by D. A. Newby, FCA, a member of Walker's staff.

28   For the foundation of Tynwald, see Wilson D.M. op. cit. chapter 5.

29 William 'Abdullah' Quilliam, was a Liverpool-born solicitor of Manx extraction, he converted to Islam and founded Britain's first mosque in 1889. He sported Turkish ceremonial dress in court and kept a fez-wearing monkey as a pet. The Ottoman Emperor proclaimed him 'the Sheik of Britain'. He died in 1932. See *New Manx Worthies*.

30 Deemster = judge

31 See Crumplin & Rawcliffe: op. cit., Chapter 10

32 *3rd Interim Report of the Select Committee of Tynwald appointed to revise advocates' fees*, para 3.7 and 3.8

33 *Proceedings IOM NHAS* Vol XI No.2 p. 172

34 Former Speaker of the House of Keys (SHK), chartered accountant, senior partner Pannell Kerr Forster (PKF)

35 Stockbroker, former senior partner R. L. Stott & Co.

36 Observed on one occasion by the author

37 For a full account of the development of banking on the Island, see Mark Solly's authoritative work *Banks in the Isle of Man*.

38 Even today, in 2008, the widely-distributed material promoting this scheme neglects to mention, apart from the unrevealing words 'after initial charges', either the up-front charges of 25% claimed by the promoters or the amount of the 'user charge' for the use of the 'rent-free properties', which was introduced as one consequence of the investigation.

39 In a letter to the author who knew him personally.

40 For much of the background relating to this period I am indebted to Julian Harper

41 For much of this and the next chapter I am indebted to the detailed study conducted by James Penn in 1999 as his Master's dissertation *The Collapse of the Savings and Investment Bank in the context of the development of the Isle of Man as an offshore financial centre* (University of Liverpool - Centre for Manx Studies), and to Dr Edgar Mann.

42 *Report of the Inspectors appointed by Her Majesty's High Court of Justice of the Isle of Man to investigate the affairs of the Savings and Investment Bank Limited*, September 1992, J. M. Chadwick, QC, Michael Jordan and John Beer (Chadwick Report).

43 Chadwick Report 23.28

44 Chadwick Report 10.42

45 Chadwick Report 23.42

46 Chadwick Report 21.4

47 Dr Mann has acknowledged with gratitude the way in which PKF switched all its resources to aid the government in this emergency

48 The task of the author; the safe was empty

49 MHK 1976; Chairman, Finance Board, 1981, Chairman, Executive Council 1985

50 See Chapter 7, pages 1 and 4.

51 May 242.

52 It took much longer for the English Institute of Chartered Accountants to strike him off.

53 May 366

54 May 276

55 May 182

56 For more information see Penn, J. op.cit.

57 J. Penn. op. cit.

58 *Chadwick Report* 23.29

59 *Farrant Report* II 19

60 *Farrant Report* III 8

61 *Farrant Report* III 10

62 *Farrant Report* III 12

63 *Farrant Report* III 24

64 *Farrant Report* III 27

65 See Acts of Tynwald 2000, pp.27-43 and 155-94

66 These addresses were subsequently published by the FSC., so proud was he of them.

67 e.g., the recent KPMG tax scheme in the USA.

68 Edwards 5.11

69 There is an Assessor's Extra-Statutory Concession which attempts to define this; the author's attempts to produce a better-defined one were not successful. A new one is understood to be pending, but has been pending for over a decade.

70 For a fuller account of the growth of the accountancy profession in the Island see *Proceedings of the IOM NHAS* Vol XI No2.

71 'There are sure to be Manx crabs'. *Manx Independent* 2nd September 1994 / *Money Media* August 1994. The second Isle of Man was given its name by one Captain John Cain, of Port St Mary, in the middle of the 20th century.

72 One former resident of the Channel Islands who came to live in the Island was the redoubtable Professor C. Northcote Parkinson, author of *Parkinson's Law*, although he probably took up residence because he had served in the army in the Island during the war.

73 *Isle of Man Examiner* Business News, 8 May 2007.

74 Nettles later rose to the rank of Chief Inspector in the TV series 'Midsomer Murders'

75 The remarks of 'celebrities' who either loved or loathed their experience here have made headlines from time to time.

76 Among the properties with which Ferguson Lacey has been involved have been Bishopscourt, former seat of the Bishops of Sodor and Man; historic Rushen Abbey; areas of outstanding natural beauty at the Sound and Langness, and the Nunnery; and, most recently, the Castle Mona, former seaside residence of the Dukes of Atholl. For those who care about the beauty of the Isle of Man and its

history, the general spread of development raises the spectre of insensitive or excessive development which all the planning and registration systems do not seem capable of guarding against. Events in Castletown in 2008 have increased the anxiety.

77   Bernard Moffatt has retired as TGWU Secretary. His enthusiasms include Manx and Celtic nationalisms. At one time Manx Radio sought his opinion on every issue, to the extent that he appeared to be a one-man extra-parliamentary opposition. But he has mellowed since the days when he proclaimed, during a petrol tanker drivers' strike: 'We will close the place down, come the Revolution'.

78   A conversation with a prominent member of *Mec Vannin* and one-time supporter of *Fo Halloo* helped form the picture of these movements' motivations.

79   Manx Star 8 - 13 July 1974.

80   Mimi, Marchioness of Queensbury, whose house was daubed when she blocked a path through her land to the beach, *Fo Halloo*, 20, November 1976 (last issue).

81   Two of them had set fire to a bungalow earlier, but on this subsequent occasion they were detected because they stayed too long on the site to burn the second house. When observed by a neighbour, they drove off in an exceptionally distinctive car.

82   It bears remembering that many of those born in the Island are not of Manx descent, while many born elsewhere are. See Appendix A.

83   For this chapter I am particularly indebted to members, past and present, of *Mec Vannin*, *Fo Halloo* and *FSFO*, and especially to Dr Susan Lewis.

84   Examples include Fern Cottage and Knock Rushen House

85   But at least it was straight...

86   There was an occasion when a man called Will Kirkpatrick parked his Rolls Royce with all four wheels on the pavement, claiming he was not on a double yellow line.

87   See appendices D and E

88   See Appendix H

89   The illustrations of buildings throughout this book together with the commentaries, provide examples of the substance of this chapter.

90   Executive Council/Council of Ministers 1970-74 and 1982-90, Speaker of the House of Keys 1990-1991

91   Council of Ministers 1986-9, Speaker of the House of Keys 2000-2001

92   One that did not find such approval was the proposal to change the title of the Lieutenant Governor.

93   See chapter 11

94   Executive Council/Council of Ministers 1982-96, Chief Minister 1986 96

95   John Donne

APPENDIX A

Appendix A

POPULATION BY PLACE OF BIRTH, 1951 – 2006 (available census years only before 2006)

Note: Figures to 1951 are census population, after 1961 resident population (net visitors)

Sources: (a) For main census figures 1951-1991 inc., Statistical Appendix, *New History, Vol.V.*
(b) 2001 from *Digest of Economic and Social Statistics, 2006*

	1951		1961		1971		1981		1991		2001		2006	
	Numbers	*%*	*Numbers*	*%*	*Numbers*	*%*	*Numbers*	*%*	*Numbers*	*%*	*Numbers*	*%*	*Numbers*	*%*
Manx-born	35,521	63.98	32,345	67.20	32,374	59.31	34,399	52.04	34,608	48.56	36,619	47.98	38,069	47.55
Born elsewhere	20,002	36.02	15,788	32.80	22,207	40.69	31,702	47.96	36,659	51.44	39,696	52.02	41,989	52.45
Total population	**55,523**		**48,133**		**54,581**		**66,101**		**71,267**		**76,315**		**80,058**	

Breakdown of Resident Population by Place of Birth

	2001		2006	
	Numbers	*%*	*Numbers*	*%*
Isle of Man	36,619	48.00	38,069	47.60
England	29,156	38.20	29,785	37.20
Scotland	2,663	3.50	2,707	3.40
Wales	881	1.20	949	1.20
N. Ireland	1,791	2.30	1,705	2.10
Rep. Of Ireland	1,774	2.30	1,705	2.10
Other EU	751	1.00	1,428	1.80
Channel Is	208	0.30	204	0.30
Rest of World	2,429	3.20	3,434	4.30
Unidentified	43	0.10	58	0.10
	76,315		**80,058**	

APPENDIX B

Appendix B

ISLE OF MAN NATIONAL INCOME – GOVERNMENT RECEIPTS

Sources:
(1) 1958/59 to 1968/69 incl: NMP Manx Year Book (MHNL Library)
(2) 1969/70 to 1978/79 incl: National Income Reports (Tynwald Library)
(3) 1970/71 onwards: Digests of Economic and Social Statistics, Tynwald Library and MNHL Library (D154)

Note occasional change in categories

	1958-59 000's	%	1959-60 000's	%	1960-61 000's	%	1961-62 000's	%	1962-63 000's	%	1963-64 000's	%
Customs Duties	2,335	66	2,391	61	2,645	68	2,649	67	2,703	66	2,815	68
Income Tax	794	23	784	20	896	23	1,045	26	1,102	27	1,017	25
Passenger Tax and Harbour Dues	17	0	18	0	17	0	0	0	0	0	0	0
Interest on Investments, & interest on and repayment of loans etc into the Accumulated Fund	108	3	116	3	103	3	0	0	0	0	0	0
Fines, Fees etc	265	8	625	16	237	6	0	0	0	0	0	0
Misc Receipts	0	0	0	0	0	0	252	6	315	8	294	7
TOTAL	3,519	100	3,934	100	3,898	100	3,946	100	4,120	100	4,126	100

	1964-65 000's	%	1965-66 000's	%	1966-67 000's	%	1967-68 000's	%	1968-69 000's	%
Customs Duties	3,260	67	3,572	67	3,583	63	3,822	61	4,264	60
Income Tax	1,226	25	1,416	26	1,729	30	2,010	32	2,324	33
National Health Service Contributions	0	0	0	0	0	0	0	0	0	0
Passenger Tax and Harbour Dues	0	0	0	0	0	0	0	0	0	0
Interest on Investments, & interest on and repayment of loans etc into the Accumulated Fund	0	0	0	0	0	0	0	0	0	0
Fines, Fees etc	0	0	0	0	0	0	0	0	0	0
Misc Receipts	371	8	363	7	375	7	441	7	479	7
TOTAL	4,857	100	5,351	100	5,687	100	6,273	100	7,067	100

Appendix B

ISLE OF MAN NATIONAL INCOME – GOVERNMENT RECEIPTS

Sources: (1) 1958/59 to 1968/69 incl: NMP Manx Year Book (MHNL Library)
(2) 1969/70 to 1978/79 incl: National Income Reports (Tynwald Library)
(3) 1970/71 onwards: Digests of Economic and Social Statistics, Tynwald Library and MNHL Library (D154)

Note occasional change in categories
Continued.....

	1969-70 000's	%	1970-71 000's	%	1971-72 000's	%	1972-73 000's	%	1973-74 000's	%
Customs and Excise	4,879	58	5,135	53	5,872	57	6,744	54	7,912	51
Income Tax: Residents	2,600	31	3,299	34	3,195	31	4,505	36	5,839	37
Non-Residents	319	4	355	4	370	4	322	3	499	3
National Health Service Contributions	172	2	231	2	198	2	228	2	233	1
Passenger Tax and Harbour Dues	0	0	0	0	0	0	0	0	0	0
Interest on Investments, & Interest on and repayment of loans etc into the Accumulated Fund	244	3	351	4	311	3	340	3	756	5
Fines, Fees etc	0	0	0	0	0	0	0	0	0	0
Misc Receipts	207	2	282	3	372	4	319	3	362	2
TOTAL	**8,421**	100	**9,653**	100	**10,318**	100	**12,458**	100	**15,601**	100

	1974-75 000's	%	1975-76 000's	%	1976-77 000's	%	1977-78 000's	%	1978-79 000's	%
Customs and Excise	9,184	49	12,132	52	13,883	50	15,466	46	17,500	47
Income Tax: Residents	7,229	38	8,282	35	10,541	38	13,915	41	16,300	43
Non-Residents	619	3	652	3	825	3	926	3	850	2
Company Registration Tax	48	0	129	1	144	1	117	0	220	1
Land Speculation Tax	0	0	97	0	119	0	125	0	130	0
Post Office (Philatelic Bureau)	304	2	517	2	428	2	609	2	600	2
Interest on Investments	977	5	868	4	1,118	4	880	3	950	3
Other Receipts	555	3	676	3	871	3	1,892	6	980	3
TOTAL	**18,916**	100	**23,353**	100	**27,929**	100	**33,930**	100	**37,530**	100

Note: Inclusion of the above years in later Digests for comparative purposes show some variation (due in part to new divisions)

Appendix B

ISLE OF MAN NATIONAL INCOME – GOVERNMENT RECEIPTS

Sources: (1) 1958/59 to 1968/69 incl: NMP Manx Year Book (MHNL Library)
(2) 1969/70 to 1978/79 incl: National Income Reports (Tynwald Library)
(3) 1970/71 onwards: Digests of Economic and Social Statistics, Tynwald Library and MNHL Library (D154)

Note occasional change in categories

Continued......

	1979-80 000's	%	1980-81 000's	%	1981-82 000's	%	1982-83 000's	%	1983-84 000's	%
Customs and Excise	24,911	49	29,525	51	34,155	51	35,125	50	40,183	51
Income Tax: Residents	18,978	38	21,699	37	24,694	37	29,279	41	32,144	41
Non-Residents	1,542	3	1,355	2	1,540	2	1,409	2	1,587	2
Company Registration Tax	311	1	681	1	537	1	917	1	906	1
Land Speculation Tax	359	1	412	1	278	0	76	0	81	0
Post Office (Philatelic Bureau)	996	2	603	1	650	1	268	1	0	0
Continental Shelf	328	1	493	1	2,993	4	1,684	2	2,485	3
Interest on Investments	2,106	4	2,200	4	1,246	2	1,914	3	1,585	2
Other Receipts	907	2	1,278	2	1,496	2	275	0	333	0
TOTAL	**50,438**	**100**	**58,246**	**100**	**67,589**	**100**	**70,947**	**99**	**79,274**	**100**

	1984-85 000's	%	1985-86 000's	%	1986-87 000's	%	1987-88* 000's	%	1988-89 000's	%
Customs and Excise	43,229	51	43,352	49	47,716	48	51,913	47	59,524	48
Income Tax: Residents	33,397	40	36,676	41	41,029	41	47,000	42	53,635	43
Non-Residents	1,581	2	1,778	2	2,741	3	4,700	4	4,944	4
Company Registration Tax	1,275	2	1,327	1	1,457	1	300	0	26	0
Land Speculation Tax	38	0	-10	0	3	0	0	0	0	0
Post Office (Philatelic Bureau)	0	0	329	0	268	0	213	0	141	0
Continental Shelf	2,763	3	2,786	3	1,129	1	1,200	1	796	0
Interest on Investments	1,714	2	1,794	2	2,097	2	2,450	2	1,773	1
Other Receipts	214	0	952	1	3,116	3	3,137	3	3,492	3
TOTAL	**84,211**	**100**	**88,984**	**99**	**99,556**	**99**	**110,913**	**100**	**124,331**	**99**

*probable, not actual

Appendix B

ISLE OF MAN NATIONAL INCOME – GOVERNMENT RECEIPTS

Sources:
(1) 1958/59 to 1968/69 incl: NMP Manx Year Book (MHNL Library)
(2) 1969/70 to 1978/79 incl: National Income Reports (Tynwald Library)
(3) 1970/71 onwards: Digests of Economic and Social Statistics, Tynwald Library and MNHL Library (D154)

Note occasional change in categories

Continued......

	1989-90 000's	%	1990-91 000's	%	1991-92 000's	%
Customs and Excise	66,552	46	70,803	43	81,541	45
Income Tax: Residents	62,333	43	79,109	49	85,624	47
Non-Residents	7,468	5	7,233	4	8,361	5
Company Registration Tax	10	0	10	0	16	0
Land Speculation Tax						
Post Office (Philatelic Bureau)	201	0	257	0	242	0
Continental Shelf	688	0	750	0	599	0
Interest on Investments	2,361	2	1,200	1	1,163	1
Other Receipts	4,223	3	3,739	2	3,898	2
TOTAL	143,836	100	163,101	100	181,444	100

	1992-93 000's	%	1993-94 000's	%	1994-95 000's	%	1995-96 000's	%	1996-97 000's	%
Customs and Excise	85,049	44	86,775	46	103,172	51	105,304	50	134,053	54
Income Tax: Residents	88,464	46	79,616	42	82,307	40	84,714	40	92,666	37
Non-Residents	8,225	4	15,141	8	9,982	5	12,382	6	13,078	5
Company Registration Tax	2	0	3	0	1	0	**0**	0	**0**	0
Post Office (Philatelic Bureau)	157	0	273	0	250	0	250	0	250	0
Continental Shelf	614	0	863	0	779	0	669	0	43	0
Interest on Investments	6,199	3	4,861	3	5,872	3	7,832	4	8,632	3
Other Receipts	3,834	2	779	0	977	0	902	0	948	0
TOTAL	192,544	100	188,311	100	203,340	100	212,053	100	249,670	100

Appendix B

ISLE OF MAN NATIONAL INCOME – GOVERNMENT RECEIPTS

Sources: (1) 1958/59 to 1968/69 incl: NMP Manx Year Book (MHNL Library)
(2) 1969/70 to 1978/79 incl: National Income Reports (Tynwald Library)
(3) 1970/71 onwards: Digest of Economic and Social Statistics, Tynwald Library and MNHL Library (D154)

Note occasional change in categories

Continued.....

	1997-98 000's	%	1998-99 000's	%	1999-2000 000's	%	2000-01 000's	%	2001-02 000's	%
Customs and Excise	137,439	52	155,939	52	183,322	54	221,905	57	299,932	64
Income Tax: Residents	92,004	35	113,872	38	135,837	40	141,591	36	142,200	31
Non-Residents	24,147	9	28,001	9	15,859	5	25,068	6	20,137	4
Company Registration Tax	0	0	0	0	0	0	0	0	0	0
Post Office (Philatelic Bureau)	250	0	250	0	500	0	500	0	1,003	0
Continental Shelf	0	0	0	0	0	0	0	0	0	0
Interest on Investments	11,076	4	1,253	0	2,380	1	2,495	1	1,840	0
Other Receipts	800	0	1,165	0	1,109	0	1,101	0	1,065	0
TOTAL	265,716	100	300,480	100	339,007	100	392,660	100	466,177	100

	2002-03 000's	%	2003-04 000's	%	2004-05 000's	%
Customs and Excise	251,561	62	306,230	66	325,786	68
Income Tax: Residents	135,260	33	134,205	29	135,452	28
Non-Residents	18,437	5	18,847	4	15,239	3
Company Registration Tax	0	0	0	0	0	0
Land Speculation Tax	579	0	293	0	175	0
Post Office (Philatelic Bureau)	0	0	0	0	0	0
Interest on Investments	1,808	0	1,978	0	2,355	0
Other Receipts	1,102	0	1,062	0	1,153	0
TOTAL	408,747	100	462,615	100	480,160	100

APPENDIX C

GDP PER CAPITA – IOM UK
Source: *Digest of Economic and Social Statistics, IoM Treasury, 2003 and 2006*

	UK GDP per capita	IoM GDP per capita	IOM GDP as % of UK GDP
1969/70	723	633	88
1970/71	792	632	80
1971/72	897	738	82
1972/73	999	919	92
1973/74	1,161	1,011	87
1974/75	1,345	1,220	91
1975/76	1,705	1,516	89
1976/77	2,024	1,683	83
1977/78	2,300	1,838	80
1978/79	2,654	2,220	84
1979/80	3,049	2,522	83
1980/81	3,544	2,561	72
1981/82	3,864	2,409	62
1982/83	4,271	2,505	59
1983/84	4,596	2,670	58
1984/85	4,949	2,937	59
1985/86	5,439	3,107	57
1986/87	5,782	3,715	64
1987/88	6,335	4,222	67
1988/89	7,036	4,855	69
1989/90	7,718	5,482	71
1990/91	8,342	6,146	74
1991/92	8,584	6,608	77
1992/93	8,898	6,901	78
1993/94	9,372	7,179	77
1994/95	9,923	7,637	77
1995/96	10,375	8,150	79
1996/97	11,081	8,931	81
1997/98	11,488	9,869	86
1998/99	12,237	11,353	93
1999/00	12,881	13,022	101
2000/01	13,442	13,922	104
2001/02	14,906	14,714	99
2002/03	15,614	15,908	102
2003/04	16,391	17,309	106
2004/05	17,451	19,228	110

1970/71 – 1981/82 inc: data from *National Income Report 1986/87* (Tynwald Library)

1982/83 – 2003/04 incl: From *Digest of Economic and Social Statistics, IoM Treasury, 2003 and 2006* (downloaded from www.gov.im)

APPENDIX D

MANX NATIONAL INCOME: INCOME GENERATED FROM BASIC SECTORS (at Factor Cost)
Sources: Isle of Man Government Income Reports, 1975 to 1991/92

	1969-70 000's	%	1970-71 000's	%	1971-72 000's	%	1972-73 000's	%	1973-74 000's	%	1974-75 000's	%
Manufacturing	6,960	22.8	5,778	8.5	6,656	17.9	6,950	14.4	7,528	13.7	11,377	15.9
Finance	3,770	12.3	4,688	5.0	6,280	16.9	8,306	17.2	10,978	20.0	18,246	25.4
Tourist Industry (1)	5,303	17.4	4,795	5.3	5,309	14.3	6,730	14.0	7,592	14.5	9,393	13.1
Construction	2,522	8.3	3,048	9.8	3,892	10.5	6,107	12.7	6,937	12.6	6,383	8.9
Agriculture, Forest & Fisheries	1,219	4.0	1,073	3.4	1,697	4.6	3,119	6.5	2,184	4.0	1,483	2.1
Public Administration	1,003	3.5	1,118	3.6	1,352	3.8	1,376	2.9	1,540	2.8	2,242	3.1
Other Services (2)	9,674	31.7	10,733	34.4	11,951	32.0	15,612	32.3	17,837	32.5	22,586	31.5
	30,451	100.0	131,322	100.0	37,137	100.0	48,200	100.0	54,596	100.0	71,710	100.0
Net income from abroad in total and as % of GNI	2,574	7.4	2,273	6.6	3,237	7.8	3,651	7.0	4,075	6.9	4,790	6.3

(1) includes tourist accommodation and a proportion of public utilities, distributive services, catering and miscellaneous services
(2) includes professional and scientific services, and a proportion of public utilities, distributive services, catering and miscellaneous services

	1975-76 000's	%	1976-77 000's	%	1977-78 000's	%	1978-79 000's	%	1979-80 000's	%	1980-81 000's	%
Manufacturing	11,410	12.7	13,479	3.1	14,508	12.6	19,180	13.7	22,155	14.1	24,998	15.5
Finance	22,997	25.6	26,905	26.1	33,447	29.0	37,138	26.5	33,808	21.6	37,209	23.0
Tourist Industry (1)	12,283	13.7	12,476	2.1	12,468	10.8	16,042	11.4	18,986	12.1	16,225	10.0
Construction	7,989	8.9	9,703	9.4	10,941	9.5	11,932	8.5	15,081	9.6	15,800	9.8
Agriculture, Forest & Fisheries	1,231	1.4	2,539	2.5	3,234	2.8	4,855	3.5	4,060	2.6	2,329	1.4
Public Administration	4,187	4.7	4,603	4.5	5,079	4.4	6,418	4.6	8,619	5.5	11,629	7.2
Other Services (2)	29,812	33.2	33,465	32.4	35,690	30.9	44,680	31.9	54,000	34.4	53,312	33.0
	89,909	100.2	103,170	100.1	115,367	100.0	140,245	100.0	156,709	99.9	161,502	99.9
Net income from abroad in total and as % of GNI	7,315	7.7	8,057	7.5	8,478	7.1	9,321	6.5	10,297	6.2	14,632	8.4

Continued.... MANX NATIONAL INCOME: INCOME GENERATED FROM BASIC SECTORS (at Factor Cost)
Sources: Isle of Man Government Income Reports, 1975 to 1991/92

Appendix D

	1981-82 000's	%	1982-83 000's	%	1983-84 000's	%	1984-85 000's	%	1985-86 000's	%
Manufacturing	22,830	14.3	23,572	13.3	27,284	14.5	31,304	15.2	32,727	14.7
Finance	34,964	21.8	36,280	20.5	39,121	20.8	39,841	19.3	48,012	21.6
Tourist Industry (1)	16,618	10.4	19,293	10.9	21,264	11.3	25,078	12.2	25,654	11.5
Construction	13,719	8.6	17,892	10.1	18,127	9.7	19,210	9.3	19,582	8.8
Agriculture, Forest & Fisheries	3,648	2.3	3,949	2.2	5,202	2.8	5,887	2.9	6,152	2.8
Public Administration	12,444	7.8	13,389	7.6	14,059	7.5	14,687	7.1	15,238	6.9
Other Services (2)	55,981	34.9	62,500	35.3	62,635	33.4	70,366	34.1	74,870	33.7
	160,204	**100.1**	**176,875**	**99.9**	**187,692**	**100.0**	**206,373**	**100.1**	**222,235**	**100.0**

(1) includes tourist accommodation and a proportion of public utilities, distributive services, catering and miscellaneous services
(2) includes professional and scientific services, and a proportion of public utilities, distributive services, catering and miscellaneous services

	1986-87 000's	%	1987-88 000's	%	1988-89 000's	%	1989-90 000's	%	1990-91 000's	%	1991-92 000's	%
Manufacturing	37,711	14	41,369	13	43,188	12	50,074	12	52,911	11	56,174	11
Finance	67,534	25	82,870	27	104,500	29	132,975	32	163,901	34	181,958	35
Tourist Industry (1)	26,649	10	28,465	9	31,625	9	32,951	8	32,227	7	33,700	7
Construction	22,297	8	26,400	8	30,105	8	35,818	9	36,285	8	36,463	7
Agriculture, Forest & Fisheries	6,941	3	7,171	2	7,561	2	8,018	2	8,675	2	9,019	2
Public Administration	16,914	6	18,775	6	20,840	6	23,132	5	26,300	5	27,620	5
Other Services (2)	91,438	34	105,612	34	126,251	35	137,713	33	158,041	33	173,124	33
	269,484	**100**	**310,662**	**99**	**364,070**	**101**	**420,681**	**101**	**478,340**	**100**	**518,058**	**100**
Net Income from Abroad	31,576	12	37,603	12	44,961	12	52,025	12	64,101	13	71,054	14

Appendix D

Continued... MANX NATIONAL INCOME: INCOME GENERATED FROM BASIC SECTORS (at Factor Cost)
Sources: Isle of Man Government Income Reports, 1975 to 1991/92

	1993-94 000's	%	1994-95 000's	%	1995-96 000's	%	1996-97 000's	%	1997-98 000's	%	1998-99 000's	%
Manufacturing	59,885	11	64,396	11	65,140	10	76,449	10	80,981	10	82,738	9
Finance	198,187	35	218,010	36	242,212	37	271,723	37	320,414	39	396,792	42
Construction	34,870	6	35,404	6	36,498	6	42,230	6	44,587	6	54,993	6
Agriculture, Forest & Fisheries	9,541	2	9,606	2	9,548	1	11,112	2	10,726	1	11,853	1
Public Administration	32,703	6	34,548	6	36,127	5	38,354	5	40,850	5	45,725	5
Professional and Scientific Services	83,911	15	92,362	15	98,827	15	109,606	15	124,015	15	137,575	15
Tourist Industry (i)	35,093	6	36,195	6	37,887	6	40,618	6	42,135	5	46,255	5
Other Services iii	114,424	20	121,913	20	131,276	20	142,953	19	149,045	18	169,658	18
	568,614	101	612,407	102	657,515	100	733,045	100	812,753	99	945,589	101
Net Income from Abroad	73,301		64,080		66,333		67,273		81,714		70,590	

	1999-00 000's	%	2000-01 000's	%	2001-02 000's	%	2002-03 000's	%	2003-04 000's	%	2004-05 000's	%
Manufacturing	79,033	7	76,665	6	97,956	7	98,883	7	114,052	7	138,949	8
Finance	448,150	41	505,382	41	494,715	37	539,996	38	551,090	36	599,806	35
Construction	71,846	6	89,600	7	115,650	9	134,631	9	145,736	9	139,928	8
Agriculture, Forest & Fisheries	16,172	1	15,824	1	17,656	1	17,808	1	18,891	1	19,013	1
Public Administration	49,967	5	53,566	5	57,205	4	63,202	4	70,173	5	75,085	4
Professional and Scientific Services	167,442	15	186,056	15	202,902	15	227,101	16	247,960	16	305,775	18
Information and Communication Technology	19,153	2	27,449	2	34,136	3	38,395	3	44,219	3	43,080	3
Tourist Industry (i)	61,438	6	67,744	6	72,451	5	74,168	5	85,544	5	97,518	6
Other Services (iii) (iv)	192,377	17	196,387	16	233,872	18	233,049	16	269,040	17	290,086	17
	1,105,578	100	1,218,673	98	1,326,543	98	1,427,233	99	1,546,705	100	1,709,240	100
Net Income from Abroad	59,048		43,447		50,691		48,386		53,930		63,267	

(i)   Tourist accommodation, with proportion of public utilities, distributive services, catering and misce laneous services
(ii) Public utilities, distributive services, catering and miscellaneous services less proportions assessed under Tourist Industry
(iii) Percentages have been rounded and so may not sum to 100
(iv) Differs from table given in *Digest* as totals for Info. & Communication Technology have been extracted separately from IoM Income reports and totals adjusted accordingly

APPENDIX E

3.3 EMPLOYMENT BY INDUSTRIAL SECTOR 1951-2001

Industrial Sector	Number in Employment													
	1951	%	1961	%	1971	%	1981	%	1991	%	1996	%	2001	%
Agriculture, forestry, fishing	2,542	11	1,911	10	1,433	6	1,412	5	1,240	4	938	3	543	1
Manufacturing: food and drink	694	3	435	2	538	2	733	3	448	1	711	2	970	2
Manufacturing: engineering	882	4	620	3	1,215	5	1,501	6	1,159	4	1,511	5	1,035	3
Manufacturing: textiles, clothing & footwear	743	3	621	3	599	3	395	2	322	1	256	1	188	0
Manufacturing: other, mining & quarrying	804	3	513	3	759	3	838	3	1,419	4	1,084	3	992	3
Construction	3,073	13	1,664	9	2,755	12	2,921	11	3,404	11	3,372	10	2,512	6
Gas, electricity and water	616	3	465	2	504	2	496	2	513	2	462	1	515	1
Transport and communication	2,180	9	1,875	10	1,750	8	2,300	9	2,437	8	2,688	8	3,331	9
Wholesale distribution	(3,315	(14	672	4	845	4	867	3	851	3	781	3	728	2
Retail distribution	(	(	2,411	13	2,696	12	2,687	10	2,993	9	2,911	9	3,644	9
Insurance, banking, finance and business services	357	2	370	2	760	3	1,515	6	4,353	14	5,941	18	8,959	23
Professional, educational, medical and scientific services	1,576	7	1,702	9	2,690	12	3,737	14	5,438	17	6,081	18	7,296	19
Tourist accommodation	(4,605	(20	(4,344	(23	1,451	7	987	4	856	3	765	2	743	2
Other catering and entertainment	(	(	(	(	687	3	996	4	1,403	4	1,156	3	2,116	5
Miscellaneous services	(	(	(	(	1,954	9	2,530	10	2,849	9	2,768	8	2,373	6
Public administration	1,870	8	1,250	7	1,134	5	1,625	6	2,144	7	2,147	6	3,105	8
Not stated or inadequately described	0	0	146	1	372	2	324	1	0	0	5	0	0	0
Total	23,257	100	18,999	100	22,133	100	25,864	100	31,829	100	33,577	100	39,050	100

Notes:
(i) Percentages have been rounded and so totals may not equal 100 in all cases
(ii) Changes have been made to the definition of some industrial sectors
(iii) Figures collected in Censuses of the Isle of Man population
(iv) 2001 figures include Information and Communications Technology sector

Source: Treasury, Economic Affairs Division

APPENDIX F

7.4 SCHEDULED PASSENGER DEPARTURES BY CATEGORY 1996-2005

	1996	1997	1998	1999	2000
Period Visitors Staying In Paid Accommodation	140,784	161,142	163,114	157,322	152,847
Period Visitors Staying With Friends and Relatives	76,666	84,188	94,438	102,170	96,920
Isle of Man Residents	219,367	228,218	244,793	263,406	301,204
Business People	71,452	80,980	76,751	74,620	79,814
Day Trippers	10,246	11,681	10,163	7,521	9,859
Total	**518,515**	**566,209**	**589,259**	**605,039**	**640,644**

	2001	2002	2003	2004	2005
Period Visitors Staying In Paid Accommodation	95,948	113,978	114,207	120,270	115,107
Period Visitors Staying With Friends and Relatives	105,345	117,165	127,814	120,688	110,619
Isle of Man Residents	329,388	346,519	346,145	343,552	360,216
Business People	76,311	87,536	88,385	92,658	88,651
Day Trippers	9,459	8,081	7,012	7,286	6,614
Total	**616,451**	**673,279**	**683,563**	**684,454**	**681,252**

Notes: (i) Scheduled departures exclude cruise passengers, visiting yachtsmen and some charter flights

(ii) Prior to 1998 figures were based on passenger arrivals, and from 1998 onwards the figures are calculated using passenger departures.

Source: Treasury, Economic Affairs Division.

APPENDIX G

7.1 REGISTERED TOURIST PREMISES 1996-2005

	1996	1997	1998	1999	2000	2001	2002	2003	2004	2005
Premises	468	454	453	443	426	391	396	382	395	414
Bedrooms	4,471	4,285	4,182	4,116	3,732	3,496	3,388	3,265	3,159	3,146
Bedspaces	9,348	8,870	8,565	8,503	7,638	7,261	6,937	6,702	6,467	6,373
Serviced	239	233	231	228	206	185	183	169	173	169
Bedrooms	3,638	3,493	3,411	3,367	3,003	2,829	2,709	2,593	2,504	2,459
En Suites	2,116	2,172	2,202	2,305	2,207	2,172	2,124	2,118	2,111	2,085
Bedspaces	7,443	7,190	6,975	6,948	6,089	5,786	5,525	5,338	5,131	4,971
Self Catering	206	197	199	190	194	180	187	187	193	218
Units	432	402	394	383	368	343	346	335	321	344
Bedrooms	833	792	771	749	729	667	679	672	655	687
Bedspaces	1,905	1,680	1,590	1,555	1,549	1,475	1,412	1,364	1,336	1,402
Hostels	8	7	7	7	7	7	7	7	10	7
Campsites	15	17	16	18	19	19	19	19	19	20

Source: Department of Tourism and Leisure, Registration and Grading Commission.

APPENDIX H

12.3 HOUSE PRICES 1996-2005

	Annual Average House Price (£)	Annual Median House Price (£)
1996	84,161	70,000
1997	95,511	76,000
1998	103,689	83,000
1999	119,422	98,650
2000	143,054	125,000
2001	157,934	139,500
2002	176,699	159,000
2003	200,520	182,500
2004	217,439	195,000
2005	231,441	205,000

Notes: (i) The median is the price level such that exactly half of the houses sold in that year were sold at a higher price

(ii) 2005 figures are provisional

Source: Treasury, Economic Affairs Division

INTERVIEWEES

John Apsden	Director FSC
Douglas Bolton	Son of Sir John Bolton; chartered accountant
Tony Brown	Chief Minister, MHK
Charles Cain	Banker, former MHK
Jim Cain	Chartered accountant, formaly senior partner Pannell Kerr Forster and Speaker of the House of Keys
David Cannan	MHK, formerly Treasury Minister
Valerie Cottle	Journalist, formerly editor *Manx Star*
John Crellin	Advocate, formerly senior partner Cains
Bill Dawson	Formerly Treasurer of the Isle of Man
Philip Dearden	Chartered accountant, PKF
Roy Callow	Chartered accountant, PKF
Phil Gawne	Minister for the Department of Agriculture, Fisheries and Forestry, formerly FSFO, MHK
Donald Gelling	Formerly Chief Minister and Treasury Minister, MHK, MLC
Julian Harper	Chartered accountant, founder of SIB
Terry Lang	Formerly Chairman of *Mec Vannin*
Dr Edgar Mann	Formerly Chairman of Finance Board and Executive Council
Peter Farrant	Formerly Vicar General
Martin Moore	Advocate, formerly senior partner, Dickinson Cruickshank
Mark Moroney	Advocate, formerly director of SIB
Brian Mylchreest	ADC to governors Dundas, Garvey, Stallard, Paul
Jim Noakes	Banking Supervisor, formerly director FSC
Roger Sims	Senior Archivist, MNH
Mark Solly	Chartered accountant, formerly Assessor and director FSC
Dursley Stott	Stockbroker, formerly senior partner R L Stott & Co
Peter and Stella Thrower	New residents
Richard Tucker	Chartered accountant, formerly director IFTC
David Vick	Director, Insurance & Pensions Authority
Sir Miles Walker	Former Chief Minister, MHK, MLC
John Webster	Formerly Government Economist

BIBLIOGRAPHY

Belchem J. (ed.)*A New History of the Isle of Man Vol V The Modern Period 1830-1999*, Liverpool 2000

Birch J. W. *The Isle of Man: A Study in Economic Geography* Cambridge 1964

Bullock, Hannah *History of the Isle of Man* 1816

Crumplin T. & R. C. Rawcliffe *A Time of Manx Cheer – A History of the Licensed Trade in the Isle of Man* Douglas 2002

Edwards A. *Review of Financial Legislation in the Crown Dependencies* 1998

Kinvig R. H. *The Isle of Man – A Social, Cultural & Political History* Liverpool 1975

Moore, A. W. *A History of the Isle of Man*, vol. 1 1977 Manx Museum and National Trust

Penn J. *The Collapse of the Savings & Investment Bank in the context of the Development of the Isle of Man as an Offshore Financial Centre* (unpublished) MA thesis – Centre for Manx Studies, Douglas

Quilliam L. *Surnames of the Manks* Douglas 1989

Rawcliffe R. C. 'The Development of Professional Accountancy in the Isle of Man': *Proceedings of the IOMNH & AS XI No2* 2001

Solly M. *Government and Law in the Isle of Man* Douglas 1994

Solly M. *Banks in the Isle of Man* Douglas 1995

Solly M. *Anatomy of a Tax Haven I* Douglas 1975

Solly M. *Anatomy of a Tax Haven II* Douglas 1979

PA *Economic Appreciation* 1971

PA *Economic Survey* 1975

PA *Review of the Common Purse* 1979

Wilkins F. *Manx Slave Traders* Wyre Forest Press, 1999

D. Kelly (ed.) *New Manx Worthies* Douglas 2006

The Isle of Man Government Annual Reports & Review from 1987

The Isle of Man Government Estimates of Receipts and Expenditure 1927 – 1962

Digests of Economic and Social Statistics, from 1975

Report of the Economic Development Committee of the Council of Ministers on the Recommendations contained in the Report from the Central Economic Strategy Unit entitled *Prosperity Through Growth.*

Chadwick Report: *Report of the Inspectors J. M. Chadwick QC, Michael Jordan and John Beer,* 1986

Farrant Report: *Report of R. H. Farrant and W. M. Hyde,* 1982

May Report: *Report of Anthony May QC,* 1991

Background Reading

Industrial Archaeology of the Isle of Man Bawden et al, Newton Abbott 1972

The Isle of Man Kinvig R. H. (3rd edition) Liverpool 1975

The Isle of Man – Celebrating a Sense of Place Robinson D. & McCarroll V. Liverpool 1990

Vikings in the Isle of Man Wilson D.M. Arhus 2008

Profile of the Isle of Man Winterbottom D. Ramsey 2007

Manx Star

Manx Independent

Isle of Man Examiner

Fo Halloo Free Manx Press

New Manx Worthies Douglas 2006

Ministerial Government, the First Twenty Years, Kermode D. Douglas 2009

Government Statistics

The Isle of Man and Britain - Controversy, 1651-1895, From Smuggling to the Common Purse Gawne C. Douglas 2009

Manx Memories and Movements Norris S. Douglas 1994

INDEX